HOPE'S
JOURNEY

A true story of
adversity, discovery and understanding
in one woman's search that led her to God

HOPE'S
Journey

LESLIE BENTLEY-DRURY

Palmetto
PUBLISHING GROUP

Palmetto Publishing Group
Charleston, SC

Hope's Journey
Copyright © 2018 by Leslie Bentley-Drury
All rights reserved

First Edition

Printed in the United States

ISBN-13: 978-1-64111-121-8
ISBN-10: 1-64111-121-6

Guided by a simple star on the home-made map, I found the road I was looking for and within minutes turned onto a long winding lane still dusty from the dry days of summer. Soon a cluster of tall pines brought a gentle bend to the left and within the blink of an eye the fenced paddock came into view. Just as I had expected. Two horses with other things in mind paid no attention as I swung by and came to a stop just short of the side door to the house.

Carol was on the porch even before I had stepped out of the car, smiling a welcome through the bright October sun.

A few words and she took me through the sunroom and beyond the soft cushions of a warm den, into a large but inviting kitchen where she pulled out a chair from beneath a wooden table. I quickly came to see this would be the place we would engage in conversation; the place where her story would unfold and finally come to life in the pages of a book. It would be a book that would carry through its length the pain, anguish and uncertainty of a journey that brought her into another place as she came to know God for the first time. And this is her story.

Chapter One

ONCE UPON A TIME IN MY LIFE

I SHALL BEGIN WHEN A MAJOR EVENT took place some fifteen years ago, and as a new century played its card onto the world stage. It was a moment when everything was coming to a head in a young unfulfilled life, forcing a woman to make choices and decisions that would eventually lead to dramatic changes and ultimately affect her very existence.

Carol's story is unusual. It is both powerful and moving and as different as it should be from any other individual experience. As it unfolds, we move through the twists and turns of a journey through such a critical part of her life where those crucial early years begin to reveal a truth that puts the struggle into perspective, and a long awaited understanding. So I will take you back to that time when the world held its breath as if in sympathy with a child of circumstance as a young woman's life was brought to the brink of despair and destruction. But as I do, I can still hear the voice of Carol across that table; gentle and soft, yet with a poise tempered by the raw exposure to a very personal battle; a woman deep in thought as the events of her life were about to be disclosed. She began to unfold the details of a time lived in hopeful anticipation, and behind a veil of her own particular adversity.

"Do you remember," she said almost wistfully, "when those years ago there was the millennium celebration, and even Mount Etna erupted before the summer really started?" she added, hesitating. "Of course in reality neither of these played any part in what I had wanted to tell you. But I wanted my story to be told. And that's about where I think it should begin. I suppose those happenings, as spectacular as they were to the world, only serve to give an approximate time to when and how my life began to change. But the truth is, and if you are searching for detail in this most unusual journey - in the lives of each and every one of us there is an actual time or date that rightly demands its fifteen minutes of fame. Or if you prefer, its time in the sun. For me, that preeminent moment was February 15, 1999. But for the sake of convenience, the months through that winter closed-in on the heels of some rather major events that unfolded onto the world, and I have used them simply as a frame of reference for convenience over the years."

She looked across at me in anticipation of my understanding; of being in sync with a truth that flowed effortlessly from her as she presented me with the unusual beginning. And I listened until her words whispered a sincerity and openness I perhaps wasn't fully prepared for - until my own thoughts harmonized with the consciousness of her personal experience over those critical years. And soon my pen would move to describe the events leading-up to this most significant time in her life, and all that was to follow from the lessons learned.

I saw clearly what she was saying. It did indeed help set a place and a time for what was about to be told. And while not directly related, as it happens, there was a logical error occurring as the year 2000 came upon us with an unexpected surprise. As 1999 ticked its way into a new year it was to be significant in many unexpected ways. It was thought a so-called roll-over into the new century could confuse the algorithms that had been so carefully expressed in the world of the digital computer partly because the last two zeroes would not be recognized as a valid year. It promised to be catastrophic if some of the popular pundits were right. In fact, to many the problem with dates within a system; four digits or two, ultimately loomed out of all proportion, threatening a new type of event horizon borrowed from the realm of General Relativity. And the world would never be the same again. But that was in the field of technology, yet the reality of our individual existence is far more sinuous than that; revolving around the affairs and the daily challenges of the human condition. This is where Time and all the collected moments blend into a ball of emotion that each and every one of us is left dealing with; the fallout of the decisions we make on our journey through Life.

Over those months and into the millennium, while the thought of a global computer collapse played itself out on the evening news, the reality of prevailing human problems seemed at times to slip under the wire. Headlines jumped from one thing to the other, while individuals struggled to survive; reaching with eager fingers to grasp and claw at the shifting shale of happiness. But beyond the steel and plastic of the modern age, personal crises were run-out along the avenues of a daily familiarity and the very Main Street of Life, reminding one of an old but superbly crafted series that once brought individual drama to the screen. They were tales of personal ordeals, suggesting "There are eight million stories in the city". Beneath the surface of one's everyday experience, that is indeed the reality. And that was the greatest truth of all. Although a metaphor for the struggling masses wherever they are, it underscored the challenges of the human condition in any setting; with situations often hidden among the intrinsic hostilities of survival in this modern age. But recent history has seen changes, and while the public scrambled to understand the problems of the Y2K bug, Carol was just one of the countless people dealing with issues of a very personal nature; where a simple mistake could shatter a dream and result in the death of an opportunity that God had planned for her life. Carol's life in many ways was hanging like a thread in this real world of Monday to Friday; traffic jams and parking lots and the occasional siren screaming a reminder to the closeness of danger. This was the real world of flesh and blood.

Shortly before what was to unfold as a turning-point in her life, and as a hard-working manager in a large corporate office, she had her mind set on a successful career. She found a rewarding satisfaction in her job and its challenges, and had done well, catching the attention of those in the executive suite. It was obvious to them she had enormous potential and drive. Things then were on the move and clearly she was upwardly mobile and ready for even greater things. She had shown enormous ability and character, along with an initiative that was essential to any enterprise. With her work-ethic and determination, she also embarked on a program in Business at an elite university and remained fully committed to the four years of courses and their exhausting demands on her time and energy. And this was attempted while still working full time, meeting the class needs of the program in the evenings. She was totally dedicated to completing her education, realizing the immense impact it could have on her climb up the corporate ladder.

With her focus and tenacity, she graduated with a degree in Business. It was a remarkable achievement, and totally natural for anyone having reached that plateau to look forward to a well-earned break. She would be scuba diving; a sport she had come to love, and for her there was no better way to celebrate all she had accomplished over those years of study. Besides, the rest and change would re-charge the batteries before she once again poured herself into the increasing demands of her career. And so, she embarked on another trip south to enjoy her chosen sport, with the added benefit of clear warm waters and unparalleled opportunities of undersea exploration. It offered something different and exciting in terms of disengaging from the pressures of her northern home turf. Carol, now in her thirties would head to the deep blue waters of the Caribbean whose warm summer days have a way of soothing the senses - far from the maddening crowd and the stress of management demands and other more personal expectations. She deserved every moment of it, and was naturally eager to take advantage of the chance to get away for a while.

Her husband had other interests and wants. He didn't dive and had little interest in the sport, and so she went alone, excited, and anticipating an incredible experience in the unique freedom of life below the waves. She had in fact been in that part of the world before, but this was to be a special occasion; one carved out of a growing desperation to find meaning and purpose in her personal life as well as the joy of a much-needed vacation. In the depths of her Being, with all other things aside, she was missing that one very special component; one that had reduced this season of her journey to an almost empty existence. She was in reality adrift in the ultimate existential vacuum that gave no rest or reprieve. Something deeply imperative was missing in her life, causing an insecurity that had plagued her since a child, filling her with self-doubt, uncertainty and growing apprehension for the future. Much as she had tried, she couldn't possibly explain how her life had been gradually slipping into an exercise of self-preservation. In the very centre of who Carol was as a woman, she was markedly alone, and struggling with a deepening apprehension. Perhaps the most significant jewel in that shining box of anxieties she would open in the quiet of a long night was one that was driving her forward. She needed to know and feel the total and unconditional love of another. To know 'it' was hers. And hers alone. She needed to know that to that special loved one, she was all he would ever need. In truth it was the only way she could feel safe. And it was at the time, all the comfort she ever desired. The successes at work essentially only masked the painful moments in her personal life, and sadly there was no-one she felt she could trust to share the feelings with.

For the moment, her waking hours were choked with self-doubt; her world prostrate with ambiguity and uncertainty. The reality was, at this phase in her marriage, the security and even perhaps the total commitment just wasn't there - or it was in question. Through the days and nights she was filled with misgiving, and no matter how much she tried, suspicion and mistrust held her in its powerful grip. It was a constant struggle to find and feel safe in her relationships; loved and needed. There would be the voices and comments heard and dismissed; to strive to be all she could be. But in the reality of the occasions lived and experienced, she wanted to still her mind: to let it free-fall into a sea of tranquility. And surely there could be no better place than sailing and diving beneath the waves of a Caribbean paradise.

Perhaps while away she could search for understanding that would in the end give her the freedom she had longed for; to know herself, and who she was; to recognize and accept the intimacy and even the vulnerability of her own needs. In the lunacy of a world gone mad with the dance of cheerless souls, anxiety, stress and the hysteria of secular life, she yearned for peace and a joyful heart; acceptance and trust. In the end, she could only hope for a time of discovery, where she could finally come to know and feel the love not only of others, but even more importantly, the love of herself. But of one thing she was certain, even at that early time of reflection. She knew whatever she must do to live her dream, she could not do it alone.

Carol was carrying something with her that day; the day she boarded the plane and set-off for the vacation she had waited so long for. She was carrying in her very Being, a history of a young life exposed to unusual abuse and discredited circumstance with all the bruises, hurts and scrapes they would leave in their wake. At that moment in time she was only pretending to be a young woman at peace, and satisfied with the choices she had made. She was, in her heart and soul lost in the forest, not knowing which way to turn. Afraid of the dark. Without direction and ill-prepared for the wilderness of human experience that would demand the very breath of her. She was a woman whose childhood bed-time fairy tale may just well have been "Once upon a time in my Life." There was a beginning to her story, - even the usual and expected conflict before the dream could unfold. But on the final pages there was nothing. And she would have fallen asleep in a halted innocence, waiting anxiously for the ending she wanted - and that would never come. It would never be read by mom or dad - only in the silence of her own mind when a young girl laid her head down on the pillow. It would be read by no other person than herself. And it would echo in the emptiness of her thoughts, and not be shared.

Carol's early life had been traumatized through an unusual set of circumstances and situations, all of which contributed to how she would see and make sense of the world around her. They also shadowed how she choseto address the challenges faced through those early years whose explanation would drive so much of her life through the unfolding of her journey. But even into her adult years, she was to experience the uncertainty of situations most might not even imagine. Consequently, many of the decisions made were in response to the stresses of childhood experiences, culminating in her early use of alcohol to deal with her feelings and insecurities. The sense of growing-up not being or feeling loved drives a spike into one's very being and causes attitudes and behaviours that are often not constructive.

Before she was out of the seventh grade she was already using alcohol to cope with the difficulties that confronted her. It would, she believed, help relieve her of the conflicts she dealt with even at that young age. Perhaps it would numb the feelings that left her confused and insecure. In truth, a loveless life knows it's own pain and perils, and she would question the reason why it was so. She would question a mother's and a father's emotional narcissism, no matter what it's cause. She was the child. And if mother, or even father couldn't love her - then how could anyone else? Over time the fall into dependency of both drink and tobacco - and later life-styles, would take their toll on a young woman trying to get into step with the world she was growing into. But there would be times she would stumble and fall. Sometimes because of the choices she made. Other- times because of circumstance.

The intensity of those feelings; feelings of loss and regret and also the lack of self-love often result in the taking of drastic steps when opportunity shows itself. And that is exactly where Carol found herself that day when she headed south into a climate that was warm and full of promise; pregnant with hope. And as wrong as it was, out of all that gripped her through those moments, she would in her weakened humanity fall prey to feelings of a desperate need. Perhaps, just perhaps, it could be erased from her memory as time passed. That would remain to be seen. But Carol had prepared herself well for this trip, cultivating an early interest in becoming a proficient and licensed diver. And the warm climate to the south; thoughts of sailing the Yucatan Channel on into the islands were both romantic and psychologically inspiring. It would be the chance of a life-time. Arrangements for travel and other details were taken-care of, and she was soon on her way to paradise.

It was on this trip into that blue-watered wonderland she met Landon for the first time; a fascinating and attentive man, and captain of one of the vessels she found herself on. Soon he would cast-off into an adventure neither could have ever anticipated. But with a gentle and easy-going nature and captivating charisma, he represented a totally different life than she had known before, and light-years away from the one she was living. They were immediately attracted to one-another. For Carol, now caught-up in this relationship with a man she had met on vacation, this exciting life under a different setting became the ultimate escape from a reality that had grown increasingly unsatisfying and empty. But she still found herself unable to let-go of a past that denied her the necessary emotional independence she needed to find and feel secure. As a result, from her position of feeling wounded and even incomplete, the marriage she was in encouraged no applause and no celebration to satisfy the inner self. It rolled out of the marital bed on a cold morning, running silently alongside the rest of her life. She felt strangely alone in the partnership, like someone clapping with one hand. The cheerleaders; friendly supporters, imagined or real were gone. And all that remained; all that was real was a feeling of increasing detachment and a growing anxiety. It was this merciless and unrelenting conflict she would be leaving behind. In its midst she found herself desperate for an 'out'; for someone or something to throw a life-line before going under for the last time. And in Landon she believed she might have found it.

There is a certain magic to the sense of wholeness we recognize as our unique personality; complete somehow in a special creation that should not be analyzed into its parts. And when a dream has been shattered, as was hers, and a mind left to rummage through the pieces, the magic is gone, and the person is left a fragment of the real self. But the search for acceptance and a satisfying sense of unconditional love strangely answers the question being asked when we begin to explore those feelings. When we come to understand this desperate need, we see that in finding that love, we come across the comfort of knowing something other than ourselves is real. And that in itself is a rewarding revelation.

As the search for that special fulfillment continued through this new venture, so did the drinking, and her dependence on it. Drinking had become for Carol the essential stimulant, helping her escape the memories and the reality of a still unfulfilled existence; of a marriage in some ways missing the cornerstone of the institution: trust. It was for her, lacking the full emotional consummation she desired through every fibre of her body. As much as she tried, she was not feeling complete. There was an emptiness she was not able to fill no matter where she looked. When she allowed herself to think of it, her mind bruised with the reality of a repeated cycle in her life. In fact, her needs in one sense were simply normal and perfectly natural. She wanted only to feel the experience and the closeness of a total commitment she could trust. But there existed a confusion about how to give; how much of herself should she invest in another. Within herself there was always the misunderstanding of how to receive in a way that would leave her feeling confident and truly cared for. Sadly, she would return repeatedly to her old fears when stressed, re-membering her early relationships, and how she had learned from a very young age that if you give all - mind, body, soul and sex - in return you will be given "love" - or some recog-nizable likeness.

Over time she came to realize how it all fell short of the real thing. She would come to know there is far more involved in any shared experience to make it real and satisfying. To be fulfilled and complete requires a different level of understand-ing; a different awareness of the intimacy a woman needs. And in fact, also a man who is emotionally honest and open. But it takes time. And sometimes pain. Tragically, and with thoughts unchanged, the giving of all of her was a pattern she would subscribe to for a very long time, suffering the hurts and disap-pointments that came with it. And there was always a payback. She believed the affection and attention from men and partners was always insincere; a forgery or facsimile of the real thing. A manufactured affection designed she felt, to satisfy a man's psychoneurotic sexual ambitions. That was her belief from another time, and on into the present. That's how it appeared to a young woman struggling to survive the challenges of a relationship in question and under its own unique stresses.

There seemed no common ground on which to meet to resolve the anxieties and insecurities that plagued her. In fact, the stresses increased as time moved-on, and to meet the uncertainties of a marriage still in its young state, she continued to lean on alcohol to give her strength and relief; an anaesthetic for the pain that would allow her to face each day. She had to feel secure and needed. But the cost was taking a frightening toll.

As it happened, Carol had a great deal of experience dealing with the issues of alcohol and its devastating effect. So many of those around her as a young girl had fallen victim to its power and influence, resulting in numerous catastrophic occurrences that rippled through the family with tragic consequences. Sadly then it was a habit she had been all too familiar with through those early years growing-up. Now its use was controlling her own life, causing her to arrange the days around the bottle she had come to depend on for her very existence. Even the hours at her office didn't escape the abuse. In fact, the stress had become unmanageable without it, with reserves secretly hidden and sips taken to relieve the anxiety and the hurt; the monotony of dealing with a life that was unraveling around her. And she knew it. She knew somehow she was playing dice with her very soul, yet trying - or pretending not to care where the cards may fall; putting the consequences of her actions out of her thoughts. At times she even wondered the point of winning the game; wondered if in the end it was even worth the struggle. Carol was weakening emotionally, feeling drawn and damaged by the daily adventure into the maze she had engineered to help her survive.

Without the intoxicating effects of alcohol she knew she could not handle life in any other constructive way. Not at this point anyway. It was a terrifying awareness for her as she pushed through the days with feelings deadened to the reality, waiting and almost expecting to stumble. With thoughts playing their usual game, she at times felt incapable of even meeting the needs of a mutually responsible relationship, should that situation ever develop. The bottle had become her closest friend at this formidable time; a friend she could trust, but certainly her confidence in others would take a back seat through this journey. Drink was good. And without it; without that glass in hand waiting to be lifted, the world became a dirty place.

Chapter Two

IF THOU MUST LOVE ME, LET IT BE FOR NOUGHT EXCEPT FOR LOVE'S SAKE ONLY

(Elizabeth Barrett Browning)

WHILE MOST OF THE BURDENS THAT PULLED at her were complicated and difficult; deeply personal, in the Caribbean she continued the relationship with Landon, whose affection and attention would relieve the anxiety that seemed to describe her marriage; one that was increasingly starving her of any true feeling of being loved, and where any sense of belonging was absent. Perhaps it was that special bonding she felt was missing; a closeness that only comes when the awareness of an uncommon love for someone sweeps into your heart with all its power and wonder. But that kind of love seemed only to be there for others. Perhaps in the depths of her silence she felt she was not entitled to that special kind of joy or happiness. Perhaps she was afraid of how she would meet the challenge if it were presented. And perhaps, should the occasion arise, she entertained a fear of failure given her present condition of coping. While she struggled to maintain a daily control of situations around her, the moments of sobriety through the quiet hours brought with them more uncertainties and feelings of insecurity. She was in the darkest of places; suffering, seeing glimpses of a reality that flashed on and off down the corridors of confusion, not knowing which way to turn. Down that hall, name-less doors would be locked, and the only way out was to keep moving in the same direction.

Through an unfolding set of circumstances, she had programmed her life to handle the pressures that had pushed their way into her experience. Keeping-up the pace and the energy would be staggering as well as dangerous. Again she needed an out - and a break from the stresses that enveloped her. She thought with certainty she had found it in the arms of a man who related so well to the woman that she was. She was finally understood and at ease with this man of the sea who leaned boldly into the Trade Winds of his own personal adventure. He was in love with Carol. And she was in love with him. The truth of it all is that Love; real Love has no reason. It doesn't occur out of intent or even desire. It happens. Unfolds and envelops us when one's passion or sentiment surrenders itself to another; a narrative of perhaps the greatest human need. And as is always the case, even vacations must come to an end, yet the growing attachment to Landon was something she found unusually fulfilling; something she didn't want to end. It had to continue somehow.

The arrangement to meet in a small town in northern Ontario was a natural next step in ensuring there would be another time to be together; to continue a closeness that was growing stronger as one week moved into another. There was a new passion in her heart that Landon had released, and the experience took her away from the questionable expectations of a distracted husband caught-up in his own familiar dream. Although an element of love was already there with Dave, and always had been, it was in question and ill-defined. It floated randomly among the pressures of another intimacy that forced them as a couple to surrender any assurance of unwavering devotion. The possibility of an uninterrupted fidelity had given-up its place, leaving a wet ring of discontent on the table, as if to occasionally catch someone's attention with its presence. With Landon though she finally found herself lifted into a new place, and into a life with a new sense of security where she was loved and desired; truly needed. She was appreciated, as was he, and so their togetherness became an adventure into a romance the likes of which she had not known before. He filled her every desire like no-one ever had; sensed her qualities and attended each precious need. And, by his own interest as well as hers, showed that special awareness that helps bind the souls of lovers. He was attentive; would listen, and give every waking moment of his time. He would care; love her, and always be available to her. And that is a priceless gift for anyone to have and to hold.

To be and feel loved changes the world in ways that can be difficult to describe, and carries its own special fragrance that becomes fiercely personal. And the memories of a setting sun, the touch of her soft skin and the warm sea; of those moonlit Caribbean nights kept her going from one moment to the next when they were not together. It was a virtual paradise when they were. A dream. Perhaps the dream also of a young teenage girl in a quiet corner of Ontario a lifetime ago. But now there were thoughts of a man whose sensitivity and sensuality moved her into giving all of herself. Her focus was intense and passionate, filled with a determination to experience the wholeness that life holds for a couple so totally committed. With it came a comfort and the luxury of feeling a oneness; a priceless attachment and sense of belonging. And there can be a healing at the emotional level when falling in love so strongly, for when we do, we often come across the missing pieces of ourselves; pieces that had slipped away unnoticed so very long ago.

Now she would remember the nights, and the words whispered over a soft pillow that buried themselves into every cell of her body; the sound of his voice that took the mind out of orbit as they blended into something apart from themselves, like two bodies sharing a single soul. Their fascination for each-other was insatiable and unending. In the nights they were together, and after the love they shared freely and with intensity, she would feel a temporary peace from the insecurity of her daily life at home. He loved her in ways he too found impossible to describe. He knew he only wanted to be with her; always near her. And she with him. The force of the passion between them, driven by circumstance and opportunity seemed to anatomize into a new creation above and beyond their individuality. A separate thinking would be increasingly difficult as their familiarity grew. A new comfort developed the longer they were together. The murmurs of an intimate confession; of passion and the petition of love from the marrow of their very being slipped into a pleasure they both held dear. It was good. Real. Powerful. Yet singularly enigmatic and engorged with a purpose that was self-evident; even predictable as their time together unfolded. And recollections of the rolling deck of a boat rocked by warm tropical waters became the reason for her very existence; the fulcrum for the promise of a meaningful and lasting relationship. It was all a possibility should things continue to progress as they were. For now, he couldn't imagine life without her, and in the most intimate moments, he would whisper those thoughts and share his needs in an unashamed vulnerability. There would be long moments of silence when nothing was said. Only felt. But she would echo his words in her own mind when they were apart. Remembering. And it would give her comfort and even hope for the next step. With Landon there was something gentle yet strong, and with expectations only of a kind that would fill the heart with all that she had wanted and needed over the years.

Now, with that special vacation long over, and the smell of the beaches and the sea but a memory, the time had come to meet again during an unusually cold Canadian winter at a quiet northern Ontario retreat. All had been planned with Carol's usual thoroughness and attention to detail. She was excited, having been waiting for this chance to be together again with Landon. And she sensed it would be a wonderful time, sharing a few days with the object of her deep affection. He had changed her life in many ways, providing a relationship of substance and intent; a togetherness she could depend on and relax into while putting aside her old familiar fears. She was beginning to believe again. And she felt the love of this man in ways that made her feel complete. It was a feeling that gave her life a sense of purpose and hope. She felt validated as a woman; understood and appreciated for all that she was. And between them a mutual trust had developed, encouraged by acts of common decency and thoughtfulness that served to give added strength to their relationship. Because of this, a new self-confidence became a natural outcome for Carol. Slowly she was losing the apprehension that had gripped her so tightly over the years. In its place was a new awareness and growing determination that helped redefine her. At least for the moment.

Carol now anxiously awaited the arrival of Landon that day at the retreat. She had prepared the house and everything in it to set the scene for the man. Menu's had been thought through, and the drinks they would enjoy carefully stored; all the details of their comfort made secure. Perhaps nervously while thinking of every eventuality, the lights were dimmed, leaving the warm glow of the fire, and with candles already burning, she moved about the rooms in anticipation; remembering, always remembering the music he loved, and the exquisite voice of Andrea Bocelli, the blind multidimensional artist, as Sogno played softly into the scene. She had thought of everything, leaving nothing to chance. She knew how much it meant to him; how much this piece inspired him. When all seemed ready for his knock on the door, she found a moment to slip into her carefully chosen leopard-skin lingerie. And then a touch of magic from the bottle of Oscar de La Renta surely completed the last minute details she had fussed over. She was ready.

Chapter Three

WHEN THE MOVIE ENDS

THE DAYS PASSED BLISSFULLY WITH LANDON, FILLING her dream and imagination with everything she had hoped for. There was that same special intimacy; an unusual closeness that promised more than these few days together. Fantasies and imaginings had been shared, and there was a safety in the feelings each had exposed. There was even a trust quite unfamiliar to her which gave her a secret comfort when the night left her in the shadows, and their understanding of each-other's needs was perfectly exquisite. She felt complete with him and totally fulfilled. And the hours unfolded as they would with relaxing times out in the bush; walks and wine soaked dinners and intimate moments as they would come together by the fire, up into the twilight of his stay. It was for both the ultimate experience into a privacy engineered to engage in the fullness of what they had become as a couple, and where the last vestiges of an old life could be cast-off like linen left along the floor. At least for the moment.

By the fourth day he would be leaving, and the very thought of that left Carol already hurting and missing the man she had come to love. It no doubt had already made a deep cut emotionally in its anticipation. Further, she would question her own sense of how she might cope with his heading back; how she might feel and handle the temporary separation from the man she had become so very close to. Perhaps she realized even more fully just how much she really needed him. It was like part of herself would be leaving with him, and it was an increasingly lonely thought that would sweep over her as the hour drew closer.

When the time came, she walked in silence with him to the car. Not much was said during the time it took to reach where it had been parked. Luggage was loaded and items packed in places reserved and familiar. There would be sounds muted from the strain that pushed its way into their midst. Sentences left unfinished. Words; words said and left unsaid in hopes for another time; another place when they could be together again. There would be thoughts, and a conscious sense of holding-back; a measured yet deliberate touch before that last embrace. She must have wondered of his own thinking on that cold February day, perhaps remembering that last time they talked and loved. Dreams that had been shared would remain in places that were safe and reached only by a wishful thought in a quiet moment. Now she knew only the straining inside before he left, wanting without any scene to see and feel the last image of him before he would drive out of her life. After all, it was a possibility, and it was frightening; distressing on a cold winter day that seemed so very far from those blue tropical waters; the smell of the sea and feel of the hot sand. There would perhaps be memories of foot-prints on a distant beach and knowing the sea would have taken them back. And conversations left, lifted on a warm Caribbean breeze, bringing new beginnings to a shore with new loves and lovers. Sudden-ly the engine kicked into life and brought her back to the present - and that final goodbye.

Her heart sank as she watched him slowly pull away from the cottage. She stared into the distance until he was out of sight, and then slowly and deliberately turned back and walked into the house alone. At that moment she could not have imagined how significant his leaving was, wondering even then of the next time they would be together. It was a difficult time for Carol as she dealt with a flood of emotions related to their shared moments over the past few days, and thoughts of times in the sun that past summer. And this was to be just the beginning of the challenges that came-up to meet her over the next while.

Over the coming hours, feelings would be mixed with both fear and regret as she now had time to look over the way her life was progressing. She felt strangely motivated to think through the affair and to take stock of where it may be head-ing. Somehow, in the very chambers of her being she was fal-tering in the shadow the relationship was casting. But the sep-aration again from Landon impacted her in every imaginable way as the hours passed, and left her feeling desperately for-lorn. And separation nudges the thinking; always reminding, as the emotions and feelings of loss roll-out in front of you. It was dramatic. Sad. Almost overwhelming as she thought on his heading back to a place she had come to love; a place that had become in so many ways a part of her. Truth was, a part of her would always be there; still feeling the warm tropical breeze on her face and the freedom and familiarity of the boat that held a special place in her heart. And she grasped and held-on to that dream with every ounce of strength she had. Still, in the cold reality of a frozen February morning, it was simply another life running parallel to the real one of Carol the business woman; the highly successful manager in a large corporation with her own staff and people she was responsible for. There were in fact so many things to consider, and her mind would fill from the pressures of the once stilled thoughts that reappeared; stirred into the mix of a new reality she began to imagine. Now her life seemed as if it could disengage and careen out of control. In the growing doubt and despair that came over her, Life had no direction, and no harbor where she felt safe. She was adrift and riding a tide of emotional need and pain.

Somehow though, this liaison with her lover appeared to have unfolded in another time and place. And that is how the mind will play its hand sometimes. But which experience was real - or even right? The pressure was on for her to make choices that could change everything in her life. Forever. There had been many fun times; moments of personal exploration that helped bring some of the feelings back into focus. In some way with this relative stranger, she felt the pieces of her life were coming together again, completing the picture like the proverbial jigsaw of what she had imagined and hoped for over the years. But at times there was the guilt that would raise its ugly head when thoughts slipped out of control as they will do. In one way, still harboring feelings and memories of abuse and neglect, she felt the affair was justified given what she had been going through over those years. Surely she had earned the right to live; to have fun and express all her desires that had in many ways been denied her.

Looking back though, she realized how her decisions; the choices made caused her to slip almost out of reach, falling into a life that would cause her to trespass amongst the images and actions of a desperate and basic desire; to find the love she felt she had been missing. It was a love that was needed to fill the deep hole in her heart. She had searched through the prism of abuse and neglect and pain in a misguided attempt to create a sense of self and indeed perhaps a new reality; an identity she could hold close and call her own. Because of how the visit had unfolded, and with the reality of his leaving, there was time to reflect further before she herself headed home to a place in the heart of Ontario.

Now, the moments that had moved between lovers over the past days had been stilled; the house settling-in to the silence that filled the growing emotional vacuum. He was gone. Heading back to his own place in the sun. There seemed nothing left to fill-in the void other than the memories; the emptiness that came with its own story. The experience and harmony of those last days would at length burn themselves out too, leaving a coldness in their place. And even with the frequent flashbacks of a euphoric bliss, one senses only the hollow feeling of nothingness in the end; of moments to be faced alone.

The search for meaning in some strange way seemed to be ending, likea fantasy projected onto a screen. Carol and Landon were stars in their own movie; their own plot and script, playing out a dream that was just out of reach, and too dangerous to hold on to. In time the movie, like all movies would come to an end. And even the future with Landon was in a way already in question. She would feel as we sometimes do that out of sight is out of mind. Unless he could be with her; experience her love and the passion they shared, he might-well collect his thoughts and move-on. Again she felt unsafe and insecure; the old anxieties returning like ghosts to haunt her waking hours. For Carol, left in a deepening silence, the tears now were plentiful and laced with the hurt and pain of times stolen to satisfy a desperate need that held her captive; to love and be loved, unconditionally, as any human being will admit to if pushed. And this is one of nature's greatest driving forces; to feel special; priceless and irreplaceable. Being unique to that particular someone bestows a value that gives confidence and a great sense of worth. It validates one's very existence and helps us feel what we think, say or do is important; that we are accepted for who we are.

Over those days, the loneliness clawed at her heart when she thought on what was missing in the sometimes shallow excursion of her daily life. Thoughts and even memories play havoc with our emotions. The emptiness was returning where nothing was solid or real; feelings of the house we imagine ourselves in, wherever it may be, lay empty when you opened the door and looked inside. Now, in her mind, there would be nobody waiting for the shallow heartless woman she felt she had become. And only a loving and trusting partner can make it into a home; a place that is warm, secure and welcoming. Still, there had been times of fun and even celebration with Landon But at the end of the day, after the party was over she began to understand there was only the orphaned consequence in a biography caught-up in the search for itself. Like many of us, she needed to escape the meaningless pursuit of vague aspiration. She yearned to know and feel what was real and full of truth and meaning. Deep inside the heart of this wonderful human being, and shy of its own nature was one of the greatest of treasures we can ever uncover; innocence. But trusting through it had proven difficult over the years. Yet Innocence had held-on to her soul; a soul that was running away from itself, hanging-on to the last vestige of a very young woman until it lost its grip. The questionof purpose; the search for that undefined singularity that describes the very thing that really validates us was also missing. What is it that makes us feel that special sense of worth we need to hold onto every moment of the day? There was no answer for Carol that really made any sense. Not at this time anyway.

A couple of days passed with her having to live and work through a mind full of memories and expectations before setting off for home. It was the end of her scheduled time there at the retreat. Over the days she had known joy, fun and even times of happiness, but there always remained a level of uncertainty where matters of the heart were concerned. Fear and apprehension were a constant companion, waiting to take advantage. That's how it seemed anyway. She was in limbo; lost in a way that left her deeply unsettled and anxious. Yet it was a state she had become so familiar with. And at least in some strange way, those feelings were ultimately reduced into one of the emotions she understood well and almost had come to expect; uncertainty. Alone with her thoughts, she would look into the fire; the very same setting she had shared with Landon over the days. There was much to reflect on now. And occasionally she would stare out across the lake and over to the horizon, thinking back, remembering the world they had shared and known in each-others company. She was missing the warm embrace and comfort of Landon. He was gone.

Chapter Four

A PLACE CALLED HOME

ON THE SECOND DAY AFTER HIS LEAVING she was sitting alone with her thoughts on one of the easy chairs by the fire. It had been a quiet time for the most part and the hours had passed into early evening with supper having long been finished. Unexpectedly the phone rang and Carol was at first startled by the sound. She turned and waited in anticipation for a moment before answering. Picking-up the receiver she said "hello" with some surprise, as if asking a question - only to hear the voice of Dave her husband who was in fact only a few short hours away from where she was staying. She felt the shock of the unexpected call and was suddenly transfixed with an ugly truth when she heard his voice. Hesitating and wondering of his call, he went-on to say he had almost driven up to see her, thinking she might have been lonely at the retreat by herself. At first she couldn't answer, but his words swept over her, gripping her with fear when she thought of the circumstances surrounding her stay there. For those frightening moments she maintained her composure, entertaining the possibility that Dave already knew of this other man. Surely, she thought, it must be the case because he wouldn't have called so unexpectedly. Perhaps he was testing her; seeing how she would handle his exposing the truth about the relationship. Her throat tightened.

After they shared a few more words, Carol capped the conversation by saying how nice that would have been, trying with all her heart to make it convincing. Finally they both uttered their love for each other, finishing with "I miss you. I'll see you soon." She hung-up the receiver in a daze, not fully comprehending what had just happened.

Still standing, she could only look into the mirror on the far wall that only days before held the images of two lovers in another time and place. Now, staring back at her was a woman she scarcely knew, yet knew all too well in her sinking heart. She froze, feeling a despondency and numbness, staring into a void that filled her with dread and fear, and even loathing. In that instant, she recognized the selfishness of her existence and actions, no matter what may have driven her to those choices. She had now become that which she had hated and tried to run from for so long. She was no longer the victim, but rather the one inflicting a pain that could destroy another; her husband who had behaved throughout their marriage, free of any form of deceit. Now, her own actions suddenly reminded her of times in her earlier life where others had deceived her, forcing a perspective that resulted in the re-shaping of her life from that point on. The influence on her thinking was profound, and encouraged a level of control that might help fill her needs. The question that leapt into her mind under this new stress was, could she live out thislie, and live or even survive with the consequences. The experience, and this moment of truth brought her face to face with who she had become. And she was repulsed by it as she looked once more at her own reflection in the glass. The identity was unclear; the shape of her thoughts frightening.

She was gripped by the stark uncertainty of a new situation that promised to be her undoing. Her world as she knew it began to unravel as the minutes ticked by. She could see the two separate worlds about to collide. Fear has a way of devouring the core of your being when you are already on the ropes of life and struggling to survive. Her husband's image was impressed on her mind, and every cell of her body screamed at the thought of what she could be facing if the secret meeting with Landon was to become known. It was a fear that pricks the heart and speeds the breathing in the desperate need for self-preservation - survival; feelings that make one walk a razors edge in search of a safe place. The head now frantic, for a moment she would struggle to understand how all of this could have unfolded as it did. What series of events or circumstances could have brought her to the edge; to bring herself to look over and into the abyss of such despair. The shear terror of those collected thoughts paralyzed any guided response to what she knew she was now having to deal with. In truth, her life was literally in the balance. And she was desperately afraid.

The voice of her husband had come through the phone like a sword through her heart. Mentally she reviewed the scenes of her early concerns with her marriage, searching for clues to find reasons for the insecurity she felt; to better understand the role her actions and drinking might have played into the scene. She was desperate also to know the causes for a relationship that undermined her confidence through a continuing need to satisfy the expectations of her mate. It was complicated in itself, and made all the more difficult by the pressures she found herself under, and the time that now made itself known through the simple ringing of the phone. She too felt the absurdity of what we will sometimes do to find those moments of happiness and pleasure; to feel accepted and validated as a human being. The price we are sometimes willing to pay is staggering, yet underscores a basic human need that all too often is ignored. Every excruciating minute and every breath could still be remembered; felt and experienced over and over again with the thought of how close it came; how close to losing all she had ever dreamed of. She felt her world coming down around her, and imagined no safe place. And panic would undo any level of comfort or peace she might find. Now there had to be choices if she were to find a way out of the situation that threatened her very world. In truth, again Dave was completely innocent. He did not deserve any of this. And she was filled with a sense of her own betrayal that was almost impossible to deal with. The shame. The guilt. The anxiety that swept over her when she realized how close she had come to losing all that she really did care for. The circumstances that unfolded before her brought every concern and fear into focus; a moment in Time when the very foundations of her Life showed in the ultimate existential crisis that described the turmoil within.

To escape the feelings that overwhelmed her that night, she turned again to a bottle of alcohol that had been left on the counter the previous night and she drank. She drank to shake the disbelief of what had unfolded unexpectedly; to dull the pain and to help push away the images that threatened to destroy her. Her life could have been ripped open for all to see. And she drank until she was finished. Until she was sick from the overdose that left her a shell of her real self - until she vomited her guilt and shame over what she felt she had done.

She continued to stay at the retreat, in a place that some called God's country for a few more days. And over the hours; in the patient moments of reflection, she found herself taking stock; feeling relieved at having survived a circumstance that had admittedly been self-created. The realization of how dangerous a position she was in struck her like a bolt out of the clear blue. Had Dave suspected something? He had called his wife with the thought of driving-up to see her. And if he had done that, he would have caught Carol with the man she was entertaining; a friend who had become more than a friend she had recently connected with. There would have been no escape; no accepted explanation. Just a goodbye from the man she at last realized more and more she really did love. He was her true partner. Her confidant. Her husband. It would have been the end of a relationship that was in reality full of possibilities and hope, and so many of the things she had needed to feel accepted and comfortable in this earthly existence. She had suffered and struggled with her past, attended the pain in whatever way she could, and had come to see where she had taken the wrong turn. Surely, whatever was wrong could be addressed. If there was the will.

On the evening of that call, and over the next few days she was filled with a numbness the affair had left in its wake, and a flood of thoughts brought her to a final conclusion. A decision had to be made. And there was only one that could possibly save a marriage which she knew could so easily have been lost. In her silence she chose to end the relationship with Landon. Looking into the fireplace again, she began to think on the years that had passed; the gains and the losses. She wondered on what might have happened to her if she were to continue on as she had, strangely trapped by circumstances that seemed to bind her. In her search, she had struggled to find and build a new life; one that would give her comfort and an emotional security; acceptance and validation. But it was to be that very act of creation that now threatened to put an end to her marriage. As for Landon, there could be no more communication. Not at this time anyway. Later there would be some exchange of thoughts about their life changes over the usual e-mails. But at this moment in her life, she was eager to make that commitment, and put the past behind her. She desperately needed help. But who was there she could turn to?

Somehow her thoughts turned to God; her family, and she wondered about her father; her mother and all the entangled heartaches, and the events leading up to this moment in time. With the very weight of the emotion, she dropped to her knees there in the living room of the retreat, crying tears hot with regret and sorrow, and suffering the pain of having hurt those she was closest to. She pleaded with God, asking if indeed he was real, to either take her life or do something with it. She could not endure the pain any longer. She prayed with the desperation of a woman lost in a material world of shadows and sorrow; caught-up in the endless search for meaning. For the first time, her thinking was changing after what she had come to realize over those days at the retreat. And though it may have appeared there was little holding her shaken life together at this moment, there was hope. And she grasped at that with every fibre of her being. Yet she needed more than that. She needed understanding; needed to know why Life had unfolded in this particular way, and with those old feelings that had also filled the heart of a young girl. Over time she would finally come to know the reason why. The search she was on would roll back the moments to the very beginning of Hope's Journey. To where it all began. Carol left the cottage with the burden of those days heavy on her mind. She found herself filled with an anxiety that was almost out of control as she loaded the car to prepare for the trip home. The stresses mentally were overpowering and intense, and she would re-check the rooms with care to make certain nothing had been left. Once she was sure the luggage was secured and the house cleared, she climbed into the car, taking a moment to look back before turning the key. She would be heading south. And home. It would take three or four hours to make the trip, and during that time she was consumed with a fear that had displaced any other feeling. The guilt was overpowering, and she found herself driving unconsciously in a state of dread and apprehension, her mind filled with trepidation. What had really happened to her over those past few months? Where would it all end? And what awaited her when she would finally arrive back at the house?

After what seemed like an eternity, she pulled into the long driveway and slowly guided the car to a place not far from the side door. Dave was waiting for her on the patio. Staring out the window, she turned-off the key and the motor stopped. There was a pause and a moment of silence before she opened the door and climbed out. She stood motionless for a few seconds, looking hopefully toward the husband who'd been waiting for his wife to return. He watched her and broke into a smile as he walked down the pathway to meet her. They came to a stop. She looked once more into his face and threw her arms around his waist.

"I love you," she said, softly.

"I love you too," he whispered back. She was home.

Chapter Five

A CHILD IN SEARCH OF HERSELF

CAROL WAS BORN A LITTLE MORE THAN a week before the Spring equinox of 1962 in a rural and picturesque part of Ontario not far from Canada's capital city. It's a part of the country known for its fine crop-lands, forests, rivers and places for every imaginable outdoor activity including the hunt. But the snow that year lasted into the early part of April, and the land lay cold until this little part of the earth turned its face to the sun.

That month, astronaut John Glenn appeared on the cover of Time magazine and "Big Girls Don't Cry" topped the singles chart. "Cape Fear" hit the big silver screen, along with "To Kill a Mockingbird" and The National Broadcasting Corporation televised their first program in color. While the final season of the memorable series "The Naked City" played-out the remaining episodes of human drama, perhaps for most, that's what Life was all about; the noise of entertainment and flashing lights; neon streets and the fast foods that promised burgers for less than a buck. But Carol came into this world in a quiet corner of the country, coming home to a farm and cattle that would be a part of her very existence through those early childhood years. The comfortable homestead sat on five hundred acres of beautiful farmland with rich soil and fine grassland for grazing. In parts it was laced with trees; forested yet cultivated by a hundred years of planning and care. It was a place shaped by both nature and man; the personalities and people creating a successful family enterprise in the beginning. And there was pride in what it had all come to mean over that long stretch of time.

For the most part, for Carol those early days were uneventful, filled with the typical adventures of a young girl finding her way through the days and weeks of her new world. But while the challenges would be obvious from the beginning as the family made adjustments to adapt, for Carol of course there would be no sense of awareness of logistics, behaviors or attitudes as the weeks and months unfolded. Still, she would be responding to the feelings developed through the interactions with those around her, along with the atmosphere of her surroundings. And this as we shall see could have significant consequences for attitudes carried into adolescence. Never-the-less, the learning curve would be great over those first years, but with everyone playing their part, the newly developed routines would ideally work to make that necessary sense of cohesion a reality. For all, there would be adjustments to their own lives as they identified new ways to best accommodate the changing needs of their new situation; a new baby in the family.

Like many people, Carol had little recollection of those early times before going to school. Instead of memories of situations or events, most of her experience would be generated through the feelings she would have to deal with that would color her little world. In fact, she recalled very little of that time before school, consumed as she would have been with the task of simply growing-up and fitting-in to the family. When we casually look upon this scene, we can all imagine without any difficulty, the events the entire family would be moving through. In this case, dad had no choice in the years through the sixties but to put farming on hold to find work in construction. Inevitably this meant time away from the family during the week because the jobs were out of town. Sometimes he would be absent for several weeks, struggling in often tough and challenging environments to carve-out a living wherever he was needed. Needless to say, demands such as these are hard on a family; every single member, for a ma- jor bread-winner to be away for long stretches of time leads to a loneliness for all. There's something particularly distress- ing and pernicious about a home missing a parent. But it's not uncommon, and families have little choice but to adapt to their new reality. Typically, and sometimes depending on age, one child will handle it quite different-ly than another; some suffering with feelings of loss and abandonment. And for the adults, while father was away at whatever job would bring- in sufficient to meet the families financial needs, mother also was feeling the weightof the task of being the only care-giver available through those critical days of the week. It carried its own sort of loneliness and emptiness; its own sadness and the feeling of so many broken and unfulfilled dreams.

Mom left the house every morning, dropping little Carol off at the near-by farm of her grandparents. Even with the sheer dynamics of the situation, the stresses to survive on an emotional level while helping improve the total income to support the family were enormous. The children, all four of them would in one way or another have to deal with at least one parent being away most of the time. And mom's return in the evening would be filled with its own challenges; re-adjusting from a day at work and trying to catch-up with the pressures of a family in need. There would be chores to address, and hungry mouths to feed. And attention expected as the hours unfolded once they were home together. It is always so difficult for families who have to be separated in order to make that basic living.

Farming over those years seemed to have lost much of its richness and profit. In fact, it was during the 1950's the production capacities of pigs and cattle for example changed dramatically as more and more 'factory farms' picked-up the business. The days of the small family farms for profit were clearly numbered, and for so many land-owners in North America, it was a struggle to make ends meet. But the family pulled together with even the kids helping around the homestead with every imaginable chore. Although they may not have been fully aware of their contribution at the time, their help and input was essential in contributing to their own survival. But for the parents, the psychological pressures would have been extremely significant. Children though are famously flexible, and youth is seemingly blessed with a series of new beginnings and eternal hope. And so it was for Carol and her siblings during those early years together.

For Carol, even in that era of growing-up, television was not a high priority, except for the Disney program watched on the weekends with her father when he was home from his job. Those moments would stick in her memory; carved into her very identity as she later grew into a young woman.

But no matter which way you look at the world and all it is prepared to give, there isn't a single person about who wouldn't admit to wanting the one thing that is so precious in a young life; time with the parents you know; to be and feel fully accepted and elevated by them. We are or were all in need of moments to feel special and cared-for and adored; to feel the urgency of a childhood dream and the need of feeling and knowing someone so special believes in you; loves you beyond anything that can be expressed. How cherished it is to be singled-out as that special someone around whom the world turns. Kids; all kids need moments together that are reserved for them, and their need to feel the strong bonding of Love. And time is one way of showing and expressing the love we have for someone. We need to feel that safe harbor even when we are too young to utter those words, or even understand them. We feel it through the conversations that drop along the table and bounce off every plate and cup and into every drawer; the added whispers that can make a child feel unique and loved; the special sayings of endearment that give us that necessary inner strength to go-on. All of this unfortunately was missing as Carol grew-up, effecting her in ways that would soon be all too evident.

And there would be other disappointments: the occasions when climbing into bed you knew those words; those very special expressions of devotion didn't arrive again today. No story would be read that night either; no parting whispers of affection as the lights were turned-out. There would be no gentle touch of a comforting hand before sleep finally carried the thoughts away - at least for one more night. Perhaps tomorrow there will be a time when you are acknowledged. Recognized. Validated with the love you so well deserve.

As an adult Carol would remember again and again with sadness, looking for any early picture of her with her family. There were none. No sounds of love. No taste of that precious affection she craved. There was only a secret longing, and a feeling of not being particularly special - to anyone. One can survive. And one does. Yet it promotes an emptiness and a longing a child can almost touch. Typically through those critical formative times, kids resort to comparing their own lives to those of others to see where they belong; how they measure-up - to see and come to terms with the value placed on them as they grow. Childhood for so many is a truly difficult and challenging journey, and often only circumstance is to blame. But it still doesn't dismiss the needs a young boy or girl has to feel valued and cherished.

Although appearing like any other 'normal' home, the house stood cold, in that sense, sitting with its own vulnerability amidst the gentle fields of a northern Ontario community. There was no embrace nor welcome from the walls that wept from conversations stained with indifference. But as always, the family, like any other, worked to stay ahead of the growing needs, yet the reality of anything resembling a closeness for the children was absent. There were differences between the parents causing pressures that affected everyone as the years went by. Mom was distant and emotionally unresponsive. While she worked hard and went through the motions of motherhood, truth was, psychologically the family moved through the days in a particular isolation that comes when not feeling connected or appreciated. Carol, like others was expected to return from school and attend her chores during the week and of course on the weekends. Even the summers; the long-awaited time for a break, included the gathering and selling of vegetables they had grown. There were no questions asked. And she took those responsibilities seriously, wanting to fully please her mother, and naturally to seek and feel her approval.

Carol chose these opportunities to see if she could find a glimmer of affection from her mother; any sense she was appreciated. There was none. At least none she could feel and hold-on to. She would work at her tasks, completing them beyond what was even expected; paying attention to every detail and every request. In reality, when mother returned from her work there was no comment; nothing to indicate Carol had done a superb job. The efforts had in fact been ignored, perhaps for reasons known only to a busy parent. But to a child, the lack of affirmation meant a lack of love - or even caring. For this girl a feeling of emptiness developed over those early years that took a heavy toll.

While there was no word of encouragement or even a hug from a mother or father, there was also no comfort to be found that might salve the feeling of loss that had become so familiar.

A cold sterility clung to areas that were common to all; even one's very room, yet there was always the hopeful expectation that it could change; that words and dreams could become feelings that were real, and every gesture an expression of love and acceptance. A child can so very easily exchange the excitement of their youth and vitality for a feeling of invisibility. But for the time being there was only the sense that mom's determination and passion for work translated somehow into its own favor and good will. Yet it was a language a young child, already uncertain of herself could not be expected to understand.

Growing-up you see and know other children at school and as neighbors who seem to take for granted those little things that spell 'togetherness' and belonging; pictures with their loved ones; of precious times together as a family; the adventures of a holiday and the images of parents holding their children close, and with obvious pride. For Carol though, and her siblings, there were no celebrated birthdays. Nothing to indicate they were important and needed. Special occasions or events were not recognized, leaving a sense that issues or even moments together were of little real value. Realities such as these hurt deeply, and undermine any ability to feel cared for or special. Individually, it was dreadfully painful because you were alone with the feelings that challenged your very worth. There was noone to turn to; no-one to feel safe with. No-one to hold your hand to make you feel rooted and secure. It would of course be stressful for everyone - especially for a young child looking for someone to be in control; someone who could and would want to take charge.

Through all these phases of development as a family, parents ought to be sensitive to the emotional and psychological needs of a young child, making sure they are met as best they can. Ideally at least, that's how it should be. Truth is, adults in a working family already struggle with the stress of making a living, and the full awareness of a child's deepest needs is simply out of reach for many. People work to survive; to put food on the table and to make every effort to keep the family safe and healthy and together. Carol's parents tried so very hard to do that, even with their differences for each-other. But circumstances seemed to always get in the way. Sometimes the luxury of a loving environment takes second place for reasons that are often difficult or impossible for a child to fully understand.

During this early period, the 'wiring' or pathways of the brain develop at a rapid pace, triggered by daily experiences; activities in play and progressing relationships. This is the stage when parents need to guide, lead and educate young minds to maximize the effects of caring and trust. It requires consistency and awareness to grow a healthy mind, and how well those pathways are reinforced impacts upon the psychological health of a young boy or girl. It really is a critical time of life for the little one, being too young to recognize or deal with the levels of toxic stress; situations that may be present such as marital difficulties, neglect or abuse of one sort or another, as well as excessive use of alcohol or drugs. But they react physically or emotionally to the consequences of it. And in the end, often through observing others, develop their own unique way of coping with difficulties that arise. Sadly, for so many, there is no realistic mentor through that difficult and challenging period; no-one to show or teach the necessary and effective skills they will need as they move into adulthood.

It was only some time later, as a teenager Carol came to understand the reality behind her birth. In fact, it seems in some ways she wasn't supposed to be born. And that is a devastating realization. Doctors had told her parents that after the oldest brother was born, another pregnancy could take the life of the mother as well as the child. Within three years of those words, her mother gave birth to Carol. There were complications, as they had been warned, and close to the time, dad was approached and asked who he wanted to save if the already difficult delivery took a turn for the worse. The father's response was "mother." With the help of an emergency 'C' section, done with every element of hope, it was a success. And both mother and daughter survived.

But all things are rarely equal where the bringing-up of a child is concerned. And most parents do not realize the new addition is in truth facing one of the most difficult and frightening times of their lives. In reality, it is a time of life where the environment has a significant influence on their growing years because the period before school is a time a child learns to trust. And while it has become common place to think of betrayal or insecurity resulting from experiences perhaps during the teen years and beyond, the first handful of years with family is crucial in developing a sense of security and well-being that will serve them well into adulthood. Our early attitudes toward learning and expression; abilities in so many social areas as well as the development of self-confidence can be traced back to a great extent to those first few years with our families. But like anything else, the issues are often extremely complex, and it wouldn't be wise to self-diagnose our own behaviors unless confidently trained in that area.

Perhaps then we will never fully know the mystery of how events through those very early experiences change the way we feel about a time; those special moments that find their way into our thoughts and memory. It is such a very personal journey, and one we take alone as our individual world develops. Over that time of course, Carol would change in so many subtle yet meaningful ways. While still just a youngster, dad of course would handle the demands of the farm as well as his job, while mom, on her way to work would drop-off Carol at her grandparents who lived just down the road. The days would be spent in the comfort of their home which also happened to be the farm next to theirs. Over many of those hours she would be with her grandpa through some of his chores checking on the cattle. They would walk in the pasture and share times that impressed at least a connected love onto the young girl. She would never forget those moments. While he was a man of few words, his heart spoke for him as did his work, and for this vulnerable child, the affection was absorbed into her very being. It spoke of love. And caring. A safe place. And home. Yet it would not be nearly enough to satisfy the psychological and physical needs of a growing child.

These occasions did much to shape her early thoughts though, and she remembered the times sitting with grandpa playing checkers for hours. Or so it seemed to a young girl. There developed a new familiarity which significantly effected her own unique personality. She remembered the smells of grandma's cooking on the big stove; the aromatic smoke of grandpa's pipe, and curling-up on the cot beside the big old wood stove and having an afternoon sleep in the warmth of the fire. In the waking hours, she might play with her cousins on the hill - the mountain as it seemed then - a time of make-believe in far-away lands, and adventures that only the innocence of youth can attend. And trips into the back pasture where every exotic step led to new discoveries that sparked the imagination with wonderful things. The mind at such a time is inventive, searching for ways to expand the world of a young mind with new possibilities and limitless thoughts. Then after the play; the fun and the time with cousins when they would visit, she remembered hearing grandpa and grandma calling when dinner was ready. A simple thing looking back, but events that commit themselves to memory for they are special in their own unique way. Priceless markers along the path to maturity.

It wouldn't be long before days spent in the house would turn into days in the classroom, and even the time after school would change Carol's life forever. Because of the work on the farm and all the responsibilities of ownership; care of the cattle and a hundred other demands of her parents, she found herself again spending more and more time with her grandparents after school. It was a memorable time of life for her, and she was adored by them; loved and lifted into a special place. She felt wanted and important – to them at least. She learned later that they had in fact both been godly people; people with values and traditions; hopes and dreams for the little girl that found comfort on grandpa's lap by the old wood fire that was always lit. It heated the large two story house and he would sleep close by the stove to keep it fed. She remembered his beard, white with age, and the caring eyes that would follow her about the kitchen where they would sit. She felt safe and secure; conscious of the special part she played in their lives. These were times when her thoughts moved to other things; when a sense of adventure moved her spirit to explore more of her world than she ever had before. But still it was not 'home'.

By the very nature of life on a farm, the days spent with friends was quite limited. It meant for Carol vast amounts of time alone with her play, creating lives and circumstances outside of her own world. She created her own magical existence with the things most important to her at that time. Her world of the imagination was rich with ideas and events that surely would have reflected her inner feelings and needs. She was independent and strong-willed; determined and eager to understand the world in which she lived. And thoughts of the future must have been exciting. But there remained one thing she continued to feel was absent in her life as she grew. She needed a love she could hold on to; feel fulfilled with. And so our story moves from the outline of her early years with her family and into a situation that was to change her life forever.

Chapter Six

WHILE THE HOUSE SLEPT

CAROL WAS THIRTEEN YEARS OLD WHEN HER sister, being much older was having boyfriends over on a fairly regular basis. This of course had been the situation for quite a while. But as time went by, there happened to be one particular gentleman who quickly became a favorite over a number of weeks. Carl was a charming fellow, quick-witted and easy-going, with an open and inviting personality. He was blessed with a certain 'savoir faire' that always stood him in good stead in any circumstance. And it would give him the confidence he needed to address his own changing needs within a relationship. In fact his easy-going manner and affectionate attitude had implications that became far-reaching in so many ways. He quickly gained the trust of those he met with his open personality and engaging character.

Carl's visits to the house to see Carol's sister became more frequent over time, and during these periods the family would get to know him quite well. They felt comfortable with him, and accepted his being there, appearing in some ways perhaps even as a fully-fledged member of the family. He had become familiar to everyone, and once there would stay-over for the weekend, participating in everything the family was involved with, helping with the occasional chore and trying to be useful. But there was more lurking behind the smiles and friendly gestures of this man who was now in his early thirties, and soon they would make themselves known to one very vulnerable teen whose life was waiting to unfold into that of a young adult; one about to enter into her own exciting time with expectations and dreams that had been stored in her heart for so long.

Naturally it was a busy house. Four children and mother home after working, and Carol's father sometimes back from his job in construction for the weekend. Teenagers have their own needs; their own time-tables, and there would be much going-on over the hours. Sometimes there would be work to be done around the farm, and even shopping to catch-up with. In some cases there might be friends to see or at least catch-up with in some way. The days then would be filled with every imaginable activity making demands on each and every one of the family over those hours. Then there were things to share through the tapestry of conversation; common things of the day, and dinner to take-on, and talk of dreams and wishes; buttered bread and the sale of paint down at the hardware store. The week would be rolled-out bit by bit for all to see, and events described and moments of interest accounted for. There would be the noise of voices and laughter and sometimes the quiet remembering of a far-off hurt that wouldn't leave the mind. And Carol would watch and listen and play her part as best she might in the unfolding stories and endless plans of excited adolescent ambition. Mom would do what she always did; making sure, at least on a physical level, everything was as it should be.

Again though the desperate need for emotional nourishment and support was unattended; her ability to become involved laying fallow as an abandoned field. The silent cry for heartfelt attention continued to be unanswered through the long dry season of her youth. For the children, preparation of the realistic daily obligations of a household might go unnoticed as the hours moved toward the time for a meal for example. But it was always there; in place and made with the same distant affection of a mother overloaded with her own demands and needs after a week of labor outside the home. This then was life on the farm - Carol's farm anyway; busy and sometimes confusing. It was full of things unexpected and adrift with it's own particular loneliness for a young girl struggling to walk onto the Life's stage; waiting for the light to shine on her own dreams. In truth she would be hoping; endlessly hoping for a touch of a special love she was desperately missing. At this age she wanted and needed to be recognized and understood. She needed someone to validate her humanity; her developing womanhood; her craving for that special affection we all struggle with at times. Carol searched her heart as every growing child does, for anything that would describe her very identity; to feel the value of a full sense of self. She needed a purpose; direction and guidance. She needed to be known and recognized; loved and able to trust again.

One evening when most of the family had turned-in for the night, she found herself unable to sleep; in fact not even feeling particularly tired at all after the excitement of the day. Probably her mind was filled with events that had unfolded over the hours after supper. But it was already the weekend and school was behind her for a couple of days.

The moments of the week were filled with things the world needed; classes and lunches and empty talk of only passing importance. It was the weekend, and time for her own thoughts and issues that would come-up over those hours. There was time to relax into her own world and enjoy some private space before another Monday rolled around. On top of that, the time spent in the freedom of her thoughts at the end of a day showed a growing independence she needed to exercise. In that sense it was fun. Growing-up meant being able to make one's own decisions at least to some degree. But this night she felt restless and perhaps a little agitated with thoughts stuck in the mind as they sometimes do; situations to mull-over, with parts of a conversation still hanging-on as if waiting to be understood. The late hour seemed to encourage that sort of personal inquiry when everything is quiet. On this occasion though she decided she would stay-up for a while longer and catch-up with television before putting her head down for the night. She would take advantage of a little time to call her own.

With the lights turned-down, she headed for the kitchen, pulling-open the fridge and looking for anything that might be satisfying. There was a soft-drink - then a bag of chips she noticed in the cupboard close to the sink. She carried her snack back to the comfort of the chesterfield and curled-up, hoping to find a show on the tube that would catch her interest, perhaps even a movie she could enjoy in peace while the house slept. There was a certain feeling of personal control that came with the late hour; a growing feeling of independence for a young girl. Now, with everyone tucked into their beds, including her sister whose room she shared, Carol settled-in for some quiet moments with her thoughts and the chance of relaxing into an interesting program. The very idea was exciting and provocative to a blossoming child who was just coming to know herself.

While the family slept upstairs, her sister's boyfriend Carl had taken a room in the basement where there was obvious privacy and a certain sense of freedom at least through the hours of family bed-time. As it happened, there were certain benefits also to him having that space downstairs. And it was a situation he was soon to take advantage of. That night, some time after the others had turned-in, he found his way up the stairs and noticed Carol alone watching television. It wasn't long before he made his way into the living room, and, pausing for a moment, focused on her sitting there, full of her youth and vitality and comfortably settled into her spot. With a quick look around, he took a seat on the sofa, relaxing into the cushions by her side. There they sat for a while watching the occasional program and sharing pieces of conversation lifted from the events of the day. Carol could still smell the familiar cologne he always wore; perhaps not as fresh after the long day, but still there. Otherwise the house was still; their thoughts seemingly undisturbed. Before much time had passed however, there was growing tension stirred by the man who sat where he could reach for her as his thoughts moved toward that end.

The scene unfolded with Carl taking control as was his custom. There wasn't much said. There wasn't much need!

And it wasn't long before he casually yet skillfully coziedup to Carol, wearing only his bath robe, and she, her pj's and her pride. After sitting together for a while, and with the occasional words shared, she became aware of an unspoken intent; the shifting to where his body touched on hers. The feelings at first were strange, but perhaps by this time not unexpected. Perhaps not even unpleasant. There was a natural excitement; a curiosity and anticipation. And there is always a tendency of youth to submit to gestures - even advances from a grown man - or woman for that matter. It's always assumed they know what they are doing. They are in control. In charge. And usually it's pretty much a given you will do as suggested because they are 'older' and know what they want. Maybe even what you want. Or so they rationalize their motives over time. You will be expected to simply follow. And be quiet.

The world of the adult to a young new teen is one of fantasy and excitement; of money and power and things unspoken. And even unclean. And those would be just a few of the thoughts picked-up from the late Saturday movies they would all see over that long hot summer. Adulthood is a place of adventure; romance and prescribed sensuality. A place of competition and loose behaviour; of work and strange commitments; of music and passion; energy and uncontrolled intensity. A frightening world in many ways. But essentially, whatever the grown-ups may be about, they surely must have your best interests at heart. To a curious young girl, moments spent in this new world could be a fun time. Different and full of adventure. Now, the dynamics of the relationship though; his engagement to her sister and family friend were changing as the minutes ticked by. And the time was broken only with the occasional comment and simple conversation; idle words that needed no encouragement.

It wasn't long before he suggested they go for a walk, or even out onto the porch where they could enjoy the evening and the fresh air. There, for a while they sat and shared, exchanging thoughts until his attention became more focused. There was in fact a warmth to his nearness and his touch and a comfort she hadn't known before. She felt animated and yet safe; even secure with the increasing closeness. She remembered his turning to look at her; looking into her face without saying a word. The situation now had moved beyond the need for conversation, being left to the secrets waiting in the silence of the night.

By now she was already feeling a tension; an anticipation of what might be unfolding. And with only the raw perplexing emotions of her youth, she dealt with the blurring of an unthinkable nearness and familiarity. Through each breath, a subtle comfort was slowly displaced witha growing uncertainty because of her ingenuous naivete. Then it happened. He leaned-over and kissed her fully on the mouth; a passionate, sensual adult kiss, sending a sexually vulnerable child into a kaleidoscope of feelings that flooded her with affection and an aliveness she could never have imagined or expected. The impact on this young girl was almost paralyzing; overwhelming her completely. She felt helpless through the experience.

In some way she couldn't imagine what might be expected or even said after that moment; a happening that was tragically stolen from her – nor the time that was measured by the quickened beating of her heart. Carl appeared calm, relaxed; confident. But for Carol there were already feelings of being out of control. She could play no part in the decisions which followed; the choices pressed upon her while he manipulated her giving toward his own ends. She didn't move; her feelings confused and uncertain; anxious over the minutes with how the closeness would finish. Perhaps there would be thoughts of a young girls dreams or fantasies stirred with a child's imagination and natural anticipation of what was about to happen. She was vulnerable. Alone. Yet in some way perhaps excited this man found her so attractive. Desirable.

He continued to push further into the innocence of his victim, touching, searching and moving with determination and experience; with cunning. This was a man in his early thirties whose romantic resume spoke of a significant experience with the opposite sex. She was only thirteen years old. A virgin still, not having even reached menarche. Her world was changing rapidly, engulfing her thoughts; mixing desire with a new reality. The feelings were new, with sensations she was quite unprepared for and completely unable to deal with. There would be for her an all-consuming walk into the world of a grown woman, with all the awareness and passions of her own developing sexuality. It was a time when the senses would have been overtaken by the flood of emotions and the heightened awareness of her feelings. She was a child turning all too quickly into an adult, being totally unprepared for the fallout that would ensue. That night, while the house paid no attention to the unfolding drama, Carol and Carl were intimate.

He had seduced her at perhaps the most vulnerable time of her life. And this was to be just the beginning.

The energy; the passion and the meaning would with great effort try to resolve itself over the hours that followed. And even after turning-in to sleep, her mind would re-play the events for the longest time, into the next day and beyond. With circumstances around the home being a minefield of complicated circumstances and indifference, there was noone she felt she could share her feelings with. No-one she could trust with what had happened to her. Even at this tender age, somehow she was aware the staggering significance of this new familiarity. At first, it may have appeared an adventure; part of simply growing-up and experiencing the first taste of a sensual relationship. But there was also a bone-chilling awareness that gnawed at her in the quiet moments of the day or night. She was in fact alone with her conscience and the reality of what had really been introduced into her life and her sense of Self. The fatigue also would show later from the exhausted feelings she was left to deal with - and to try to understand. And the only resulting comfort of that evening was the sense of being loved, even under such extraordinary circumstances. Whatever else her thoughts entertained that night, she felt something unusual and unique had walked into her consciousness. She was needed. A page had been turned in her young life. And there was no turning back. So much had been experienced; life tasted at an unexpected level. But the loss of innocence would plague her for the rest of her life.

The late night meetings, and other encounters during his visits continued to happen for several months, leaving Carol sometimes perplexed yet excited by the attention he was giving her. Why would this man be so determined to be with this young girl who wasn't yet even old enough for high school? Over time she began to wonder - could it be simply for his own sexual gratification? In the end, is that all she was wanted for? His pleasure? Or was he truly in love with her as he wanted her to believe and understand. Thoughts would cross her mind at times wondering how this unusual relationship might affect her sister who was clearly in love with this man. In fact, soon they would marry. There would be guilt on some level too. Even questions of preference when she considered herself in an unwanted yet real competition with Barb. He was obviously still heavily involved and even committed with her sister, and so his behaviour and focus left Carol confused and without answers.

Carol then did not have the maturity to deal with the thoughts that came at her. And given her age, so much of what was unfolding; the dangers and the excitement would have gone over her head. She felt she couldn't talk with her mother for so many reasons - nor her brothers and certainly not her big sister. Dad also was not really available; his absence in fact encouraging an old insecurity; of not fully knowing her place in the world. In truth she was a young girl in search of herself. She wanted a sense of belonging and attachment. She wanted a place in her emotional world to call her own. And in the strange bewildering relationship with Carl, it seemed she had found it. For a while anyway.

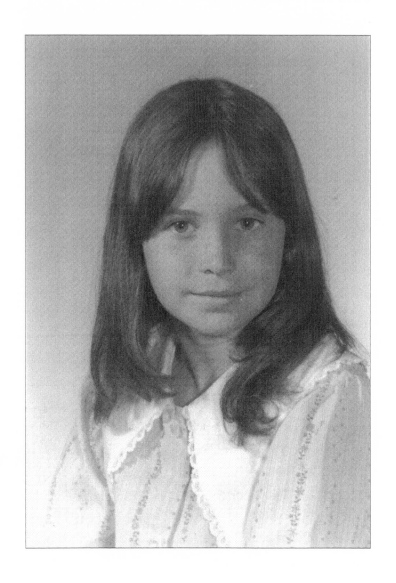

Chapter Seven

BETRAYAL

ALTHOUGH SHE MOST LIKELY WOULD NOT HAVE thought her situation through in any logical way, over time Carol questioned her sense of 'not belonging' as she struggled through different experiences growing-up. And it was a heavy feeling she was never able to shake off – though not an unusual one for an adolescent struggling to make her way in the world. But her life, emotionally was relatively empty. She was unfulfilled; searching for meaning and purpose, with no-one to turn to for advice or simple guidance; at least, noone who really knew her through those early years. Her own developing sexuality would also begin to drive her feelings, and again, she was desperately in wanting of true affection; the kind she had seen in movies or read about in magazines the girls would share at school. Even talk about amongst themselves. She needed to be wanted and important; to be singularly the love of someone's life. She wanted to know what it would be like to have someone who believed she was the most important human being on this earth. She needed in her own way, not only the love and security of attentive parents and siblings, but ideally a special relationship with someone of the opposite sex. She needed someone to feed the heart and soul of a young girl who struggled in silence, waiting for the moment she would be accepted and treasured above all-else. For the time being though, the reality was in stark contrast to what she had hoped for. And she was missing the counsel of a mother's focus on a daughter's developing imperatives; the embrace of human understanding from someone who loved her completely and wholly and unconditionally.

Because of these issues, and the early experience with Carl, as the months went by she found herself repeatedly running into the arms of men much older than her years. Perhaps she felt a greater strength in their apparent maturity; a growing confidence and esteem, and sense of acceptance. She really was needed, feeling even more like a woman; although a very young woman, in control and with a purpose. She was finally sensing her life had direction and intensity; a meaning she could hold on to as the weeks went by. Looking back, she saw Carl had reinforced his affection with words expressing his love for her. And with no counsel or experience, her vulnerability was easily overcome. It would have been obvious to a much older man that in the pubescence of her years she was naked and defenseless to the charms of such sophistication and emotional invention. And while she at times entertained doubts of his real motives, a tragedy occurred that was to impact the lives of the entire family. Her brother Ethan was killed in a car accident after a bout of heavy drinking. They were collectively devastated of course. And grief slipped its cold fingers into the lives of them all as they struggled to deal with the loss. Both parents were coming apart at the loss of a child, taken so cruelly in the prime of his youth. It was a crushing experience for everyone.

It was sad, yet this tragic event only reinforced Carol's need to again be comforted by Carl, no matter what doubts she had allowed to creep into her mind since that first experience with him. Mom was particularly overcome with the loss of her son. But it seemed any sense of parenting and concern for the remaining three children had been abandoned. There was no-one to console them, and Carol was left alone with her feelings and fears. The loss reflected back on her and her needs. She needed the comfort and security of a parent and family who could help set her world back on its axis. She needed to know life would go-on and that she would survive; that they all would survive and find a way through this tragedy together. But for this child, the only immediate way to make it less painful was to feel the love Carl was giving her so lavishly. And so the abuse continued; advantages taken with someone who was in truth quite helpless to change the direction of her early life.

As it was, he used the moments of their grief to pull Carol closer to him, and in fact, he was the only comfort she had under the circumstances. Mother became even more distant, while her father took away his pain through the bottle. He was drinking now more heavily than ever. The only safety for her through this time was in the comfort her sister's fiance was giving her. And in part, it was this particular kind of attention that started to fog her views about love and the sexuality she had been so eagerly introduced to. Is one always related to the other? Can there be love without the giving of one's very body in return? Is that what she must be willing to give if wanting affection and closeness in the future? For a young mind dealing with so much, and growing-up, it can be confusing, for no standards had been set; no expectations. There was no scale of values by which to measure all that had unfolded over this period of time. Perhaps there were no rules; no innate morality whispering its displeasure. Perhaps in the real world of grown-ups, Conscience takes its leave, giving-up its seat to Opportunity. As the months passed, she again began to sense something missing in this unusual yet familiar relationship. She was maturing psychologically as well as emotionally, and over time other things became evident. At first she dared not think of it. The scaffolding of her already fragile life was starting to shake itself loose with thoughts the affection Carl held for her, once again were probably nothing more than a pitiful excuse to fulfill his insatiable sexual appetite. Her need was desperate. But the doubts continued to consume her, leaving her with questions there were no answers for. The slow but plodding development of the awareness and sense of self was in fact frightening. The embrace of the intimacy she had experienced with this man began to unravel even further when the real purpose of the relationship pushed its way into her mind. When victimized, a girl in the end feels only objectified and exploited. Certainly not loved.

After a while she came to fully understand the picture she was a part of. Finally she was utterly convinced of his motives as he continued with every opportunity to press his affection and charm on her. But now she believed from the core of her very being he was using her. And in her youth, she knew there was nowhere to turn, nowhere to go with the hurt. Given the situation and dimension of the tragedy, she could hardly approach her mother with her grief after all that had happened to her and to them as a family. Nor her father when he was home. And her older sister of course was completely out of the question in terms of getting advice and finding comfort. And the present circumstances were certainly not the time to chance a confrontation she was ill-prepared to handle.

Again the effect of toxic stress from the early years continued to take its toll in every corner of her life. And the fact remains; the greatest gift a parent can give is, first, their time. From it, and through the care and affection they might lavish, a sense of Self grows from those family roots; feelings of bonding and belonging. An infant needs that time to develop their identity with confidence. They need to feel totally accepted and loved into a place of safety and emotional well-being; a place of self-assurance. For Carol, as for many others, the connection on that level was never made. And a child; any child takes-on the impossible task of parenting themselves through their own desperate hopes and needs. It is for all kids in similar circumstances a recipe for disaster. And for this particular girl, the experiences before and after that first evening with Carl left her with the gut-wrenching feelings of emotional abandonment as time passed - feeling in some ways, lost to the world.

Now the color of the experience she had with this older man began to change, and the feelings came with a vengeance.

Pain and anguish took over her mind as she thought on what really had been happening with Carl. Her sister had been deceived. The guilt was intense and there were moments of self-loathing with the full understanding of what she had inadvertently been a part of. She came to realize the depth of the hurt she could have caused; may well have caused if the facts became known. In the reality of it all, she saw she was, and had been in a full-blown affair with her sister's boyfriend. At the tender age of thirteen she had become 'the other woman'. She had, in the trusting moments of her age been taken and abused in a most savage way. Now that trust; innate in a young human soul had been broken. And it would affect her for most of her life, long after the experience with Carl was buried but not forgotten - along with the dreams and hopes of her youth. Over the years that followed, the effects of the relationship were to have a devastating influence on her, causing decisions to be made that were often unsound and almost desperate in order to survive. And in the wake of the affair, a pattern had been set for the way she would relate to other men in her life. In fact many years would pass before she could respond to the hurt in a positive way; before she could even begin to trust as she once had.

As Carol related her story to me across that table, her voice pressed with emotion, I glanced over her shoulder to the china cabinet and the cups and plates that came with their own memories. And there looking back at me was a picture of her as a young girl. She would have been perhaps nine or ten years old. As I peered, her voice continued, moving in and out of the moments, recalling the years so vividly, and sometimes with sadness. But now the voice came through the eyes of that young girl in the photograph staring back at me. I saw the love in the face of this beautiful child; the hope and trust she would still hold for but a little while longer. And as a father, I couldn't help but think of her being my own. I remember nodding as she related her story with detail; my pencil poised and ready to record a hesitation; a thought that may have slipped out of control, triggered by some forgotten event. And if I were to be honest, there were times when I struggled with the impact it was having on this writer. But the story needed to be told. This she wanted more than anything. And I was committed to completing it for Carol, and for the benefit of others who, so encouraged by one woman's extraordinary journey might also come to know God. There was such certainty in that hope.

Chapter Eight

DERRICK

After the experience with Carl through her early teens, Carol found herself dating boys at her school and for a while getting seriously involved with others closer in age. Like any teenager, she wanted to be seen and accepted; to be a part of the in-crowd. Competition can be fierce though those high-school years, and any self-respecting girl would want to know how they impact both the young men as well as the young women they interact with in and out of the school setting. But soon there were times when school began to mean so much more than a path to education; itself being put on the back-burner as other more personal needs pushed their way to the surface. She needed to grow; to feel alive and be a part of the larger peer group. She needed to know where she might fit-in; how she would be accepted, and the value they would place on her friendship. She needed normal relationships that wouldn't be challenged. And that would come for the most part through her interactions with others at school and dating boys her own age.

With all that had unfolded over the previous months at home, Carol's thoughts drifted away from the academic demands and into areas of life that needed a much greater focus.

And at this moment in time, the attention she sought revolved around boys as well as other girls, and how they would relate to her; what they could give her in terms of the deep needs that continued to grip her. Although I'm sure sought-after by her peers, she herself believed otherwise, adding no doubt to a lack of self-confidence and esteem. Pressures from this alone would influence the thinking in such a negative way, causing her to make choices not in the best self-interest. But times were about to change for Carol. And in a way she hadn't expected.

Derrick rode into Carol's life like James Dean, straight off the set of "Giant". He was handsome and appealing; self-assured and confident of the fact he attracted attention. His blonde hair and tall strong frame swept into Carol's life at a critical moment in her mid-teen years. She was immediately attracted to him; his voice and affectionate personality. He seemed at first a very gentle man, warm, kind and soft-spoken. She would give him the attention and the intimacy he needed; pushing her affection into the soft corners of his personality and enjoying a unique and comforting familiarity. But he also gave back, and his voice, in its calmness brought one to catch his words; his thoughts. Wherever they would move about town, he was proud to be with her, and he showed it with the warmth of his touch and an obvious closeness he demonstrated openly and even in public. But with his character already scarred, the bold bodacious hand-crafted cowboy boots, finished in a natural tan only underscored his individuality in a quiet statement to the world. He was a man comfortable in his own skin; relaxed. Independent; even tending toward being a loner. He'd learned from an early age that to get his own needs met, he had to be somewhat aggressive at times, showing he was in control. And if something developed to challenge his level of comfort, he could swing into a different gear with a particular temper. Over the months, Carol would come to know all about this potential in a very personal way.

She had met Derrick in a most unusual way. While visiting a friend's apartment during a school lunch-break she passed by him on the street corner almost across from the place she would be visiting. And this became a frequent encounter over the following days. She found herself having to literally step by him each day, and couldn't help noticing his presence and attitude as he stood waiting on the corner. She was curious. Intrigued even and no doubt filled with questions. There was a magnetism to his presence, and she was quickly drawn to a charisma she sensed when near him. After one of her visits to her friend's apartment she headed down the stairs for the walk back to her school. Once out onto the road, she crossed the street to that same corner where he was still hanging-out. It was on that occasion he stopped her and made small-talk as they made every effort to connect in some way. There was a mutual attraction, and during the conversation he asked if he could see her sometime. She agreed, finding him both interesting and attractive. And mature. This was essential to Carol at this time of her life. In fact he was much older than she. Derrick was 26 while Carol was just 16. She felt flattered. Felt special in fact. He was different from the boys at school who by comparison were immature and unsophisticated. And his choice of wanting to be with her made her feel she too had really grown-up. There was a statement made when this 'older man' with unseen qualities wanted to spend time with her. Naturally, his friends were of his age for the most part, and there was something tantalizing and interesting in that too. Simply stated, they made Carol feel accepted and attractive in ways the guys in class just couldn't match. The experience with Carl was still quite recent, and through those years with that man, she had acclimatized herself to the expectation and moods of an older partner. Derrick, to some degree would follow in his footsteps over time, although in different ways, and leave a mark on Carol that would once again impact her for the rest of her life.

The times with Derrick, after a few months became tumultuous and hopelessly unpredictable. When they first met he was exciting and different; even strong in personality and protective. He was both mature and 'in control' of his life; a man perhaps many young women would fall for if given a chance. She felt safe at first with him, feeling he loved her; even needed her as she wanted to be needed. Certainly she believed she could trust him. After all, he did love her. Over the weeks that followed, a new facet to his personality began to appear as the layers of his character were slowly peeled away. Under the surface lay a cruel streak waiting to show its face; a violent tendency that raised its ugly head at times, especially when alcohol entered the picture. But there were other issues lurking in the background unforseen by Carol - and often the cause of his outrages and increasingly impetuous behavior.

Many of those early days together were spent taking walks around the town, bringing their own familiarity to the sidewalks of Main Street; the local park where they would often meet-up with friends, and drives into the country to be with each-other. Over a short period of time they became very close, and the relationship was for the most part relaxed and wonderful and fun. Early in this new togetherness she began to feel the influence of a new security which she was desperate for, and it felt good to have found someone she could be so close to. He was easy-going and even shy outside his small circle of friends, but she would notice at times his ability to become aggressive if someone angered him in any way. Still, she was naturally forgiving of such things in the beginning, feeling that overall, he was a pretty good guy. And we all carry our quirks and at times questionable attitudes; especially when challenged with the reality of everyday stresses and the need to survive in a world that appears selective with whom it shines fortune onto.

Mom, once she became aware of her daughter seeing Derrick snapped. She was adamant; unmoving, and was against the relationship from the start. She demanded Carol stop seeing him, and the situation began to take its toll on the two of them. But she continued in secrecy to see the man, and feeling a sense of happiness and hope, was inadvertently pulled-in to a life style she never could have anticipated. Derrick had turned more and more to drinking, and Carol was conveniently used to help support the habit. She found herself at times stealing money from her mother's purse and giving it to Derrick. Mother continued to insist he was a liar. A cheat; a thief, suggesting he wouldn't hesitate to even steal the cross from the church if necessary. She felt he was morally incapable of anything else and pursued her daughter with the demand she end the relationship.

For Carol, as the weeks passed, her attention became more and more turned toward the relationship and making sure it was safe. She needed that feeling of continuity and belonging, of making a difference in someone's life. For now it was Derrick, and all the baggage he may have carried with him became hers, and together they would somehow make it work. It was intense. And the more mom would push to see it ended, the more Carol was determined to see it through. The whole experience left her feeling her mother never really loved her; that in reality the actions of this parent were simply to deprive her of any level of joy or happiness. Sadly, for this emotionally hungry teenager, it certainly seemed that way to her at the time.

In the end, Carol found herself increasingly uninvolved with school. She was disengaging from all those usual expectations and perhaps earlier hopes. With no interest or encouragement from either parent, Life defined itself only as the struggle to survive on every level. The issues loomed through a growing mist of apprehension over the waking hours, leaving her with no desire; no will to finish school. The relationship then with her mother became even more strained - to the point where it ended in a terrible fight. They struck-out at one-another with their hands, landing slaps that would imprint on more than the physical body, and causing hurt and deep emotional bruising which would take a long time to heal. After this major confrontation, she was given an ultimatum. She had to stop seeing Derrick - or get out of the house.

Later that week she found herself in an identical argument with her father, culminating in a tragic episode while in the barn with her beloved horse. Dad approached, hoping to talk with her, and, with Carol assuming he had spoken with mom, a verbal fight ignited unexpectedly.

They argued, and with dad on one side of the horse and Carol the other, she reached over and struck him hard with her hand. The fallout from it all was obvious and painful to think about. Realizing that too much damage had been done to her relationship with both parents, she called Derrick. It wasn't long before he came by to pick her up. The feelings would have been extremely intense as they drove away together. And surely Carol wondered in silence where it would all end; and how she would deal with this major change in her life. Her entire future was at stake. And there was no-where to go after leaving the farm: her childhood home. Derrick couldn't even think of taking her to live with him. He himself was staying with his grandparents who she had never met. But he did resort to sneaking her into the house late in the evening, and managing to make certain she was out before others were even awake.

It was with this situation in mind that Carol approached her grandmother to ask if she could stay there for a while. Thankfully she agreed. In fact she stayed there for several months which proved to be a tremendous help. As Time played itself out though, Carol left school out of sheer necessity, with a feeling there was no point of continuing. She had to support herself, and found a job in the laundry room of a near-by nursing home. The work was hard and came with its own challenges and expectations. The little money earned ended-up in the pockets of Derrick, with the sole purpose of helping support his problem with drinking, which was already in a downward slide. It was around this time that this once gentle and thoughtful man began the horrific abuse of his sixteen year-old girlfriend. Carol was starting to see another side to her beau that might have appeared out of the pages of Dr. Jekyll and Mr. Hyde. It would become terrifying over the coming months as life took-on new challenges and pushed her into making choices she could never have imagined.

With drinking now a major part of Derrick's life, his treatment of Carol took another turn. He became increasingly abusive and violent, often beating her savagely. One can only imagine the pain she would have endured from the reckless punches and kicks. There were times he would take the boots to her literally, and she would find herself on the pavement with horrific suffering; severely battered and not knowing where she could turn. And for all intents and purposes, she was alone. All alone and at the mercy of a brutal man she had once loved, and who had loved her so openly. He had excuses, as men of that persuasion and temperament often do. His blood sugar was low, he would say, and his emotions and anger were out of his control. And so it went. But after one such terrible night, she returned home to where she was living, and a concerned grandmother saw how beaten and bruised she was from this latest assault. The next time he came to pick her up, he was confronted by her and told never to come around again or she would call the police. And she meant it.

Sometimes our needs get the better of us. We do things; make decisions right or wrong and suffer the consequences as the results unfold over time. And it was no different for Carol. She continued to see him, and at length, found herself having to leave her grandma`s house to find her own way. Given her youth and circumstances, and now as a high school drop-out, she did the best she could to survive. The stress must have been incredible. She couldn't return to her family for help, and would have known the intense pain of being emotionally abandoned and let down. A horrific beginning to a young life. The heart of this young girl must have been broken with the betrayal she felt. The emptiness and loss of trust left her hemorrhaging all hope in a whirlpool of uncertainty and despair.

Carol soon began to realize the source of at least some of the problems Derrick found himself grappling with. She found-out he was still sneaking around to see Patti, an old girlfriend she thought was long-gone from his life. But that wasn't the case at all. Their connection was still alive and well. On top of this, he not only continued to deny it when confronted, but the accusations themselves were enough to bring about another beating for her. But Carol was determined to catch him in the act. One night, with Jill, her close friend by her side, they took their bikes to wherehe lived and waited for him to come home. Thinking of how he had successfully taken her those months ago into his grandparent's house late in the evening, she naturally assumed he may well be doing the very same thing with Patti. She was incensed. Sure enough, that night as they sat waiting where they couldn't be seen, Derrick arrived home with his old flame in tow. The house was in darkness, and with everyone asleep, he snook her silently up the stairs to his room - exactly the way he had with Carol. She was overcome with anger, and again, with the betrayal and lies he had left her with.

The girls watched in silence as the light came-on in the bedroom, and then saw it turned-off. Suddenly there was a flood of memories for Carol to deal with as she remembered those same actions, when she was the one climbing those stairs with him, like a thief in the night. It left her hurting. Hurting until she could take no more. With Jill close by, they began tossing stones at the window to distract him from what she felt they were doing. With great determination and good aim, they continued 'til they saw the light turn-on again. Within moments he came running out the door, looking feverishly for whomever was causing the attack. But he didn't have to wait long, for Carol ran to confront him head-on, yelling in frustration and rage, and unknowingly putting both her and Jill in harms way. Tragically, he responded violently, knocking Carol to the ground where he began to beat her mercilessly. So much fear must have welled-up in her; again the sense of hopelessness against such odds. Finally he turned on Jill as well, hitting and kicking her savagely as he had Carol. At length, and no-doubt with hate-filled satisfaction he moved back into the house, leaving the girls to their wounds and in their aloneness, comforted only by the darkness that surrounded them. Tragically, in their youth and uncertainty, neither-one would take the chance of calling the authorities or taking the assault any further. It was a hopeless situation and so destructive to the very soul.

As surprising as it may seem, somehow the relationship with Derrick continued even after that horrific experience. Of course he would ask her forgiveness, swearing it would never happen again and insisting that he still loved her. But the cycle was predictable, and was repeated again and again. She found her thoughts confusing and her feelings bent from the abuse; and from a man who professed his love. But she also felt hopelessly controlled by her thoughts which had become distorted to the nature of what real love was all about. And the confusion is understandable given her age and the path her life had taken; her loss of innocence while still a child.

With an inner awareness that he was still in a relationship with Patti, and with the abuse continuing even after the promises, she began to realize the importance of breaking free from this man, and from what he had taken her through over the two years she was around him. In desperation, she called home one cold winter's night in the midst of a snowstorm. She asked for someone to help her; to come for her to take her home. She had to swallow her pride and even feel the embarrassment of admitting her parents had been right all along. Finally her dad said he would send someone - a friend in fact. He could not attempt it as the roads were snow-bound and impassible, and the farm was about fifteen miles out of town. The friend and neighbor who was closer to where Carol was, agreed to pick her up in his truck and take her back to his place. Once there, they set-off on a snowmobile, through and over the deep drifts to the farm. At last she was home. Safe. Free from that indescribable experience. But there would be the explanations; descriptions of her experiences with a man who now seemed crazed and out of control. It would have been a very difficult situation for Carol; the lowest point in her life and feeling totally defeated. One can only imagine the thoughts that passed between Carol and her parents, and the stress of the collected moments now she was home. The hurt was palpable. But how do you even begin to heal the wounds that had been opened over the months? How does a family begin to reconnect and make-up for all that had been said; for the decisions that had been made and the still raw feelings over broken bleeding relationships?

Suddenly someone shouted there was a man walking up the driveway. She looked out and to her horror saw it was Derrick. Someone had tipped him off. Through the heavy snow, he had driven as far as he could before his vehicle was caught in a snow-drift. From there he walked some distance up to the farm. By the time he arrived he was coughing-up blood, but was anxious to take Carol back with him. Being afraid of what he might do; concerned, knowing his ability for violence, and overwhelmed by her thoughts, she left with him, later wondering why her parents could have so easily let her go after all they had done to get her back. However, a week later, and in her struggle to survive, she had to call home once again, saying she needed help. But this time her father didn't arrange to have her picked-up. Rather, he contacted Carol's older sister and her husband who were living out of town and asked if they would take her in; look after her while she got back on her feet. He realized, wisely, that life for her in their small town had become impossible and even dangerous. So, he did what he thought he should and arranged for her bus fare at the earliest date. And soon she found herself on her way into the very heart of Ontario, and into a new life.

As a final note to this chapter, it was only a short time after moving to another town she heard that Derrick, the once true love of her life was dead; killed in a car accident. A victim of his drinking.

Chapter Nine

THE FACE OF CHANGE

WHILE DAD HAD HIS DAUGHTER'S BEST INTEREST at heart, he couldn't have imagined what awaited her in her new surroundings. He would have naturally assumed she was safe, far from her home town several hours away. And of course he had no idea what Carol had experienced in those early years at the hands of Carl. To her father, the only real problem had been her relationship with Derrick - and the violent behavior she had fallen victim to. That's what he had hoped to save her from. And one would assume her parents would have spent long hours talking-over the best course of action for their daughter. As it happened, her sister was now married to the man who years earlier had initiated a very secret affair with an underage child. With Carol. And those times of deception and manipulation; of victimization and sexual abuse were still fresh in her mind. She was at this point licking her wounds from the times she had spent with Derrick, and her senses and emotions were raw. In reality she was more weakened than ever after these almost repetitive experiences. But she had to move-on.

By this time she could no longer trust anyone. And moving to a new and unfamiliar town held particular challenges and fears for a teenager. Still, she longed for that loving touch; to feel accepted and cared-for. To feel needed and uniquely wonderful to that special someone. But her move into the city only brought her back into a setting she was familiar with from the past. Perhaps 'safe' with in some way, inasmuch-as she was aware of all the expectations. She moved-in with her sister and Carl, and being vulnerable from all that had transpired over those years, she once again fell into his grasp. Although now with considerably more awareness, the new setting seemed in some way a mirror of those earlier times when she was not really into her adolescence. Now, while in her late teens and in a strange city, she was still in a state of uncertainty and insecurity, and she once more became convinced through his words and behavior that he really did care for her. Perhaps even wanted to be with her. This time though she had perhaps the extra maturity to turn away from his advances. But could she? The times had changed, as had the circumstances, but her needs remained the same, and would for some time to come.

In my judgement, it wouldn't be constructive nor reasonable to move forward without commenting on some of the issues that would have colored her thinking after finding herself in these new surroundings. Falling back into a relationship with the same man who had confused and hurt her just a handful of years ago seems at first hard to even imagine. Yet it has long been suggested that being subjected to sex at such an already difficult period in life, with the corresponding lack of physical, emotional and psychological development will often result in unexpected consequences. There can be serious negative effects to having sex at a very early age partly because the brain and nervous system is still developing. In fact the body interprets this physical intimacy as a stressor, triggering an overdrive of the immune system and even influencing coping skills as well as levels of depression. It is complicated, but research is leading us toward that understanding. And the above obviously impacts heavily on moods and emotions, throwing a wrench into the way decisions are made and options addressed. The possibilities for more informed choices are as a result, severely limited until the issues are dealt with and understood. And only time and patience can see that happen. Answers to so many questions was to be Carol's focus over the coming years. She needed to know the "why's" of how things happened, and what part others, or even herself played in their unfolding. The victim (and she was a victim of circumstance) seeks reassurance and safety under these pressures; understanding and acceptance, and a certain familiarity. "Familiarity" can become a safe harbor when those early steps of late adolescence are taken into adulthood. It is a frightening time. And that's perhaps where Carol found herself after moving to live for a while with her sister and Carl. She was in a condition of deep susceptibility after her recent ordeal at the hands of Derrick and feeling emotionally exposed; unguarded and unprepared for what was about to unfold. Perhaps she felt she could finally trust Carl again. Perhaps in her need to feel connected and secure, she believed, if nothing else he at least understood her. He did seem to be 'there' for her when she first arrived. Perhaps he even loved her after the passing of so much time. But perhaps more than anything, she was seeking a comfort she believed no-one else could fill without giving her life or her love to another. There really are occasions where there just isn't enough time, and situations develop out of a sense of desperate need of the moment. And no doubt this was one of them.

Be-that-as-it-may, there are certain realities that help describe the decisions a late teenager may make under the duress Carol found herself with. We typically assume a young woman has an already well-developed awareness and sense of self. Even a degree of confidence. After all, they appear 'grown' and mature. Ready for the world on any level. In fact she was only part way through the developing of a mature brain with all it's expected capabilities. The pre-frontal cortex in particular continues to develop and is not really established until well into the mid-twenties. Yet we expect, socially a young female of Carol's age to be fully 'prepared' and lacking only perhaps in the realm of certain life experience. Until that time is reached, many show behaviour that is at times impulsive; even desperate. It is still a time of uncertainty and frequently even fear, and any choice that helps them reach a necessary long or shortterm goal may feel acceptable. A great deal will depend of the pressures she is exposed to or simply experiencing. Often though there may be periods where there's an inability to process emotions effectively, causing other concerns and stresses.

Successful development of that necessary sense of Self may be dependent on the history of intimate relationships. If a young woman experienced relationships with men or boys from a very early age, their own sense of Self can be, in simple terms tied basically to a man - or to each man she is with. In some cases, it may be the only way to feel validated, with any sense of virtue. In the end it is essentially a struggle for an identity; a search, and Carol's coming into a new town with new expectations and circumstances, making the right choices alone presents a number of obvious challenges. In fact, looking at the bigger picture, in so many ways, it is also expecting too much of a young woman who stepped into the world of the adult totally unprepared through no fault of her own.

So, the affair began all over again while she was still in her late teens. Later, those same feelings returned; the self-loathing and low self-worth. Although there would have been moments of satisfaction and the excitement of intimacy, somehow the heart knows and nudges us to the reality of those shared and stolen times. The man was the husband of her sister, and that fact alone was enough to trigger the intense guilt she felt; the remorse. It contributed to even more pain which seemed to pile-up in the mind and color every part of her life. There was confusion. Doubt. And feelings she was at times unable to face. One of them that stood out above all others was that of 'Victim.' She knew even then her life had no direction and took turns down avenues of secret dreams and hopes. And always searching. Waiting for an opportunity to unfold as it was, life was spiraling down and she was losing her grasp on ever experiencing any sort of normal life. There would be moments of fantasy; of imagining a closeness in that special relationship she had seen with others. But the trust had gone. And she believed in her heart she had become nothing more than a sexual tool in which men found their own gratification. She was resentful, yet at the same time needed desperately those moments with someone who might allow her, in the dark night of the soul to feel even a morsel of affection; to experience again a closeness and a tenderness. Although immensely difficult to identify when so young, a thread had been pulled in the fabric of her experience, for hidden in its own secrecy was the need to feel rooted; to feel a sense of belonging. In an almost cruel reality it's a journey that takes many their entire lives to find. And tragically, many never do.

Still, the needs had to be filled with something that resembled the touch of human love, even if the element of sincerity was absent through it all. And for her, the re-attachment with Carl was the only way to have it. It was at hand, and she gave-in to the pressures felt through a new and challenging phase of her life. With this as a yard-stick she would measure her self-worth; her intrinsic value as a young woman, and question the ability or desire of anyone really loving her. Although extreme, there are in fact times in this intimate journey when a woman may resent a man's affection, feeling her low self-esteem and his attraction to her shows all too well his own low expectations. It is sad. Tragic in fact. But non-the-less often a reality that is not uncommon in the lives of women trying to reach for the happiness and satisfaction they seek.

The situation with Carl, and the thoughts of her sister being his wife gnawed at her very being and she would know the remorse and guilt of what was happening again between them. She was hurting and didn't really know how to stop it. Her feelings were becoming more confused as time went by, and she was desperate for a change. She was incapable now of trusting anyone. But perhaps more importantly, she was tragically incapable of even trusting herself in a relationship.

It was during this time when she was hit with another major challenge which gave her also a sense of extreme loss. One evening there was a phone call she certainly wasn't expecting. Her father had fallen down the basement stairs back home and had been taken to hospital. She was naturally devastated. Over a few hours he still hadn't regained consciousness. Tragically, he had struck his head against the cement wall at the foot of the stairs and succumbed to the injury shortly after. Sadly, he had been drinking before the accident. And there was no doubt it had been caused by the effects of alcohol. It must have been overwhelming for all of them, and Carol couldn't help thinking of the death of her brother whose head struck the pavement after a car accident, caused also by heavy drinking. One can feel the hurt she would have experienced. The grief felt.

While dad was still in the hospital, Carol rushed home to be there for the family. By the time she arrived, it was already too late. Later she would think back on that time and of her move to a new town to escape the abuse of a man who was in his own way demented and debased. But she would also think back to her father and the times, as few as they may have been when he would spend those special moments with her; time on a Sunday evening with Walt Disney, or a summer afternoon by the lake where she would swim. She would remember his calling her, holding a towel to dry her after the cool water had caused her to shiver under the hot sun. She would remember.

With tragedy still fresh in her thoughts, she also dealt with the connected memories of riding with her cousin; riding like young girls ride, laughing into the wind and having the fun of their lives. And remembering dad would in the end take her to find not only a horse for herself - but two. The days in the sugar bush of grandpa's farm, and Spring when the sap was running. The together times when they would tap the trees. The making of Maple sugar, and sounds of his fiddle at the sugar bush camp when the snow would fall. The smiles and sticky cones when hot syrup poured into a handful of ice. And then now. Everything was still, except for the mind.

With so much having transpired through those difficult and painful early days, with memories still fresh in her mind, she would find herself dwelling on the events that impacted her life so strongly. She might never understand the progress of his own life and trials over that time. Perhaps no-one could. Yet, she would remember the drinking; the fighting with mom and the frustration felt through each struggle. She would recall the holes in the wall from a fist, and the hurt she felt; the loss she felt over her youth. But she would also remember his call to her. The ticket arranged for her journey into the city to be in a place that was safe. And in the end, she would forgive, and somehow know in her heart he had in his own way tried to be there for her; to have her free from the conflict of her past; to help lift her into the future. And in the final analysis, she would come to see in that simple gesture, the image of a father's hope for his daughter. In that there was some comfort. And over the years she would keep that thought somewhere safe.

She had been aware for a long time of the effects of alcohol on her family. It had been devastating; at times resulting in their living in a strange isolation from each-other, but managing somehow to present a face of normalcy in the community. The feeling that was front and center for her around this time was one that stilled her thoughts in some way. Dad had tried to help her get away from the abuse she had suffered with Derrick. In a way he had helped save her. Yet it seemed almost ironic he was not able to save himself. So, it was a time of reflection; a time to take stock and address values and think of the future - and of the changes already apparent in her life.

As time passed, and things began to level out for her in her new surroundings, she received a letter from her grandfather; the one she had spent those memorable times with as a young girl. Somehow he had heard of her struggle to start a new life; the difficulties and challenges she was facing. In his kindness and love for her, he had sent a check made-out in the amount of $1500.00. Truly a blessing for Carol at this critical time. She felt uplifted, and remembered the care she had known during the time spent with her grandparents through some of those growing years. And this generous gift would help her in many ways rebuild her broken and somewhat emotionally fractured existence. She would never forget it. Nor the feelings it left her with.

With the help of her sister she enrolled in high school which came with its own challenges being a little older than most of the others students. But she pushed through with determination and studied hard to maintain high marks. And she did. Education now took-on a new meaning and purpose. She was able to see the benefits of succeeding, and poured everything into completing her program. It gave her a renewed purpose and sense of worth; something she had been missing for so long. And in the final month of the school year, a program was already in place that sent graduating students into the community; into local businesses for one week to obtain work experience in the real world. Carol found herself with a large very reputable company working in their Human Resources Department doing basic but essential tasks. And before leaving this short assignment, she wisely submitted an application for a position with them. Although she had also been looking for placement in other industries, the one place that had given her that wonderful opportunity responded in very short order, asking if she could begin work right away in a clerical position. She was dumbfounded. Her school agreed to release her early, giving her excellent academic standing, and she began her career only weeks after completing her credits. Because of her achievement and high marks, they decided that final exams were not even necessary.

At last she was able to strike-out on her own initiative with a renewed confidence and sense of responsibility. Soon there would be no need to rely on others for her success. At last the time had come to show the world who she was and it was exciting; invigorating and deeply rewarding. At last her life would take-on new challenges and she would come to know the freedom of choice in so many parts of her life. A page had been turned, and through it she saw new opportunities that before were simply out of reach. She would finally be in control of her future, and feel the warmth of success in so many areas of her life. It had seemed like a long wait. But she had made it. Once involved with her job she noticed a new independence and inner strength as a result of all her hard work and dedication. How it would impact on her relationships remained to be seen.

Chapter Ten

THE GAME OF LIFE

OVER TIME CAROL TRIED DESPERATELY TO PUT those early years behind her. More than anything she simply wanted to move-on. The independence felt good; she was finally 'in charge' of the future at least to some extent, although still a little insecure. And this would particularly apply to her personal life and those she would invite into her inner-circle of friends or acquaintances. Part of the problem was she had no yard stick to gauge herself and others. It simply wasn't in place. And in some ways she remained unarmed and considerably vulnerable in this area of her life. Personal reflection would bring-out the old fears; fears of rejection; of not knowing fully the way a caring and loving relationship should develop should she find herself in that place. What does one really look for? How does one interact in a way that is positive and constructive? How and where do we learn to recognize true sincerity and commitment? And how much of ourselves in the beginning should we be willing to give?

It wasn't long before she met a man who lived in her own high rise apartment building in the south end of the city. One afternoon he'd called from his balcony, seeing her returning from a trip to the store, making small talk on the treat she was carrying, and clearly encouraging a get-to know encounter. Perhaps with his spontaneity and openness he caught her attention, for it wasn't long before they were talking even before the end of the day. Already so much had happened to Carol in her short life, and this casual meeting with a neighbor was a well-timed opportunity to move forward into a new beginning. Over a very short time it flared into a relationship and he was clearly deeply attracted to her. For the first time she felt someone was seriously interested in her; even perhaps in a long term relationship she could feel comfortable with. There was an obvious spark between them that drew them closer as they worked on getting to know each-other over the following weeks. Slowly they discovered things they had in common which was exciting for both of them. They dated for quite a while, doing as much as they could to be together, realizing over time they appeared well-matched as a couple. It was an exhilarating insight, leaving both with a feeling of confidence and well-being. The experience was thrilling, and they totally enjoyed each-other's company; sharing moments and interests which seemed to bond the relationship even more as the days went by.

It wasn't long before they were making plans for a vacation, and heading to Las Vegas where their togetherness really began to blossom. He treated her with great respect and care, showing a deepening affection for her as the days passed. It was satisfying for both of them and enjoyable in every imaginable way. One of the qualities she admired was Troy's attentive and thoughtful nature; showing an admiration and acceptance she had never known before. She soon found herself completely falling in love with him and longing for the meaningful future the relationship promised. After all she had experienced over the recent years, feeling safe and wanted with a man she could really love filled her with tremendous hope. She was beginning to feel also she could trust him with her feelings and even her uncertainties. After so long a wait, and with all the trials she had come through, life was finally taking a turn for the better with a promise of a loving partner and perhaps even a future where they could grow with each-other and fulfill their dreams. At last, Life was good.

But Life is full of surprises. Before too much time had passed, an issue arose that offered to destroy them as a couple. Carol was shocked at the news he allowed to filter down into one of their conversations. He began referring to old girlfriends; bringing-up issues and memories of earlier loves and losses. His last was a woman named Debra, and over a short time, she also, through his persistence would weave herself into their lives, causing a serious splitting of affection and focus. Carol was shattered. Then the final bombshell: in the emotional confusion she found herself in, Troy informed her he wanted to start seeing other women. For Carol the reality was numbing. No matter what she questioned, there were no answers to be had. And the old thoughts began to return - the self-doubts and lackof trust; the deceptions she had experienced as a young girl only a few short years ago. As a result, she started pulling away from him in the fear of being hurt any further. She worked desperately to change her interest in him and move-on. She needed desperately to put distance between them; to take stock of her life. But it would be difficult. Still, she had to try.

Through opportunities in her workplace, she joined a baseball league in the hope of re-connecting again with the world of the single woman. In the beginning it promised to be exciting, perhaps opening doors to new personal opportunities which she needed to move ahead. It would give her something encouraging to look forward to; something to channel that energy and put her back in control. And this involvement would help keep her socially busy through the long weeks, which would be essential as she worked through the most recent loss with Troy.

But the players; the men and women from work gathered not only to play the game, but also to give legitimacy to the casual meetings at a watering hole after their time on the field. The natural focus would be the connecting with others; testing the water for relationships of any kind, and making oneself known. Individual status, attractiveness and availability would be foremost as the drinks were downed, with elbows bending late into the night. These were times when alcohol flowed all too freely and loosened the inhibitions to encourage a boldness or increase the much-needed confidence; to compete for the attention of someone who would turn one's head that extra time. There would be stories told and tales enhanced and behind every conversation, a secret tallying of virtues and doubts on both sides of the table.

For Carol, after a few of these get-together's there were nights where deep personal questions would keep her awake once she arrived home. As the hours slipped by, she would struggle and re-live the conversations that had tripped on a waiting vulnerability - and perhaps question the wisdom of her openness as she worked to understand the pitfalls of people searching for a future partner. There would be thoughts of the coming week's game and other times at the bar; dreams of security and fulfillment, happiness and what we all imagine to be normalcy on the tree-lined streets of suburbia. Perhaps even the creation, meaning and recognition of a new family unit. The adventure can be exciting. Romantic in its own way. And so it should be. Yet there are always the unexpected let-downs through the experience and at times, feelings of a hopeless disappointment. Still, a young mind and heart is universally filled with Hope. And somewhere deep inside we mostly believe we will succeed in the end. But getting there is one of Life's greatest trials, and the ultimate adventure.

As it happened, those times with the guys after a game were soon to come to an end and in a way Carol would never have imagined. The get-together's had turned into the perfect opportunity for drinking; the ultimate party at the end of a day, and the time on the field. In fact, while the game itself was fun and rewarding in its own way, the main event would be for most, the chance to meet at the watering hole for their weekly time to unwind. Like so many others, perhaps Carol hadn't noticed she was consuming more than her share of drinks, and it was having an effect on other areas of her life even after those weekly stop-overs. Joining the league had brought her to meet more people than she otherwise would, and this was naturally exactly what she had wanted. But the cycle of drinking was becoming far too comfortable; far too convenient, and it dulled the senses in more ways than she had anticipated. While she could feel free from pressures and expectations of life at home and at work, the habit was impacting severely on her private life, lowering her social inhibitions to an already dangerous level, and causing her to take chances with casual relationships.

One night with friends after a game, and after enjoying the evening, she drank herself into a stupor, taking away any sense of concern or responsibility. The drinks gave her the confidence she needed so very much with the challenges she was facing, but when she left the party after some time in the bar she was not in any condition to drive. That night she didn't think twice about climbing behind the wheel of her car and turning the key. After some hesitation in the tavern, she'd managed to navigate her way into the street and finding her car in the lot, that's exactly what she did. And it brought for her yet another life-changing experience.

Truth is, of course she shouldn't have been driving at all. But she did, putting the car into gear and heading out into a rain-swept night where the roads were already slick from the wet pavement. As she came to a stop light she quickly braked, only to have the rear end of the car swerve into a pole. At this, she panicked, realizing her mistake through the fog of intoxication, and made a left hand turn through a red light. Luck wasn't with Carol the night of this terrible ordeal. Looking through her rear-view mirror she heard the sirens screaming toward her; saw the lights of the cruiser and in the fear it brought, sped-up only to realize within seconds what she was doing. In the final moments, and in a desperate confusion she simply pulled over and sank into her own hysteria, trying to decide what she could do. But the wait wasn't long. Within moments the officer approached her car and she shook at the thought he would smell the alcohol once the window was down.

She was confused and hurting; her head spinning from the effects of drinking and the hitting of the pole. Any act of rational thinking now was beyond her, and she felt numb when asked for her driver's license and insurance which she struggled to find, fumbling through her purse.

She was asked to step out of the car and walk the line; a picture so vivid to any who watched such scenes play-out in the movies. But for Carol this was real. And she was the one struggling to appear 'normal' while under the strong influence of so much liquor. For a breath-taking moment she felt she could do it; pull it off if only out of sheer determination. Perhaps the shock of the accident had sobered her up enough to convince the law she was fine. But in the stark light of reality, her head still reeling, she failed the sobriety test, realizing through a drunken maze she had lost this round - and her licence in the process. If there were any doubts, they left when the officer asked for the keys to her car, explaining the routine for such an offence. Her car would be taken by tow-truck to be impounded, and she was driven back to the station to spend the night in jail; an experience that would haunt her for years to come.

The time spent behind bars with herself brought her to think on her life and where it had brought her. Over the hours her thoughts would be consumed with far-reaching questions of the wrong turns she had taken on her journey. And there would be more to come. For now, she was drowning in the decisions she had made and looking for a way out; a way back to a life of responsibility and happiness. She wanted more than anything to lead a normal life in a normal caring relationship. She wanted to feel the security and contentment she imagined others having. She wanted to 'belong' and be accepted for who she was. But the pressures continued as her life moved-on through an almost monotonous daily grind - with times often too predictable and worn. The stresses of getting by alone; of finding success in the jungle of life in the city were enormous, and Carol at this point simply didn't have the resources to handle them. She would search for answers over the years and through each challenging situation, wondering why she could not make it as she should. Or even could. In truth, this was of course her own personal perspective; her own personalized view of a failure she couldn't even begin to understand, nor really come to terms with. It was painful. It would confuse the mind, and in the breaks taken through the day, there would be moments that would cause her to glance at the image staring back from the glass, the mirror or window she would walk by. She saw herself; a young woman traumatized by a brutality and a hurt she couldn't find a place for, and memories from those early years she couldn't seem to escape. They would haunt her through the night and shadow her decisions in the day. Always there. As if part of her. And in the vulnerable state she was in, she judged herself harshly for the choices she had made. Yet how often its been said, that the things we regret most in this life are not always what we did so much, but what we failed to do when given a chance. The very thought of it would surely color her moments through the days and weeks ahead.

In truth, Carol was a girl who had known little direction in her growing years and was ill-prepared for the challenges Life would throw at her from the very beginning. In her inexperience and basic repertoire, no sign-posts had been placed to guide her through the maze she would encounter as she worked to make a living and to find her place in the community. In essence, each decision she made was activated not through awareness or good judgement so much as it was by guess-work. Finding the right path or direction was difficult for there was no compass to guide her. In fact everything in Life had become a gamble. She knew it. And it was a terrifying thought to deal with alone. There were few about she could confide in. She had lost all ability to trust. And she was frightened. She had been deceived and misled. Used and abused by the human kind. And trust was not in her emotional vocabulary through these years.

Fortune though seemed to shine its light on her as the months went by. She met a man she liked; really liked, finding herself deeply attracted to him. She probably didn't think to question why in any detail. But that's how things seem to be with matters of the heart. Even from the beginning he seemed different and had something special to offer, and she found herself taken with his personality and nature, and surely that's enough. After all, one has to trust the feelings we get when Life seems to play another card. And if it's working, feeling-wise and moving in the right direction - toward some kind of fulfillment or satisfaction, then why even question it. Again he was an older man, coming into the picture with the apparent credentials of maturity and related wisdom. As it happened, he also had two children living with him from a marriage that was already broken, and Carol would spend time with him and the kids; a quality time where they would get to know eachother through a unique interaction as a potential 'family'. But she would have to be patient.

After several months they decided to take a trip to Florida together while his children would stay with his mother. It was a perfect situation in that sense, and encouraging for Carol. They would head to Fort Lauderdale to spend a week together, away from the busy life of work and the city with all its demands. And any unfamiliar setting is prime for getting to know aspects of someone's character and values. They would be forced into a close proximity and a certain dependency in terms of staying as a couple in a strange location. These situations always force the breaking of certain boundaries and inevitably reveal a great deal about an individual; their level of patience and care; attention to their partner and concern for the other's happiness. It would in many ways become the ultimate experiment in understanding a potentially 'significant other'. And in that sense, nothing could have been better.

Everything was going well and they were having a wonderful time in an exciting and exotic place. But after just a few days into the vacation he took Carol aside and told her he wanted to go home. She was more than surprised at his suggestion and wanted to know why? These would have been uncomfortable and painful moments. He finally responded by saying he was already missing his kids and needed to go back. Carol was shocked. Hurt. She was struck by his attitude which made her feel she was not as important to him as she had first believed. It was a tragic moment for her and left her upset and shaken. Insecure. The relationship that offered so much hope was collapsing all about her, and it wasn't long before they parted company and went their own way. But for Carol it underscored her feelings of doubt and inadequacy. She was left to question yet again why the relationship had failed. But the answers were slow in coming. Only after much thought and introspection would she come to understand how it all might have happened. Was it again in the choices she had made? Regardless she was left feeling down and with even less trust than before. And she questioned in her own mind what was yet to come. Whatever it was - would she be able to handle it?

Through a series of crushing set-backs, she began to very seriously question her judgement even more. She questioned whether it was even possible for her to enjoy a normal constructive relationship with someone. Could it be she was not reciprocating as best she could? Was she somehow holding back? Perhaps afraid of her own feelings? The thoughts would haunt her and she was afraid of any further failures with a potential mate. As much as she tried, she couldn't begin to think of what might be going wrong. Could it just be circumstantial? Possibly her own choices and decisions she had unwisely made? Jumping into situations she really wasn't prepared for? Or was it the result of a bitter cruel world of predators and those who sought only a self-gratification wherever it could be found? The hurt and doubt would haunt her and invade every area of her Life in ways she never could have imagined. It would consume her. And it seemed there was nowhere to turn for help or guidance as she struggled to pull herself out of the quicksand of these cruel threats to her happiness and fulfillment. But she had to move-on. She had to push forward into a new life and somehow manage. She had to cope using the only tools available to her; determination and hope. Truth was, that's really all she had.

Chapter Eleven

IN SEARCH OF MYSELF

FOR CAROL, LIFE MOVED-ON WITH ONE DAY; one week blending into another, along with the challenges she would cope with 'on the run' as best she could. She had to survive. Ultimately it brought her to entertain other ideas of fulfilling partnerships; alternative ways. For the most part, her experiences and successes with guys she had known had been particularly negative. They had not served her needs, except the providing of an intrinsic level of intimacy which served a purpose as the teenage years unfolded. But there was no warmth or real acceptance she could put her trust into; nothing that would describe her individuality or identity. The relationships in fact left a lot to be desired with respect to connecting to the woman she had grown into. Given the losses she had experienced over those years, and with her mind looking for something fulfilling and meaningful, her thoughts brought her to change focus in her search.

Over time a new awareness had developed, perhaps out of a certain privation of what she had been missing in her life; perhaps simply out of the excitement for that special something that would pull her attention away from the hurt that still gripped her. Regardless, and for reasons she would later think back on, she became not only interested in members of her own sex, but eventually also involved and committed. With all that was filling her mind, the confusion and lack of feeling truly connected to a world she was at odds with, it seemed like a necessary move; an experience she felt essential to her very well-being. Perhaps it came about through a wishful effort to bring a new and untried stability to her life, or answer a simple curiosity that many of us entertain. Truth is, there seems to exist somewhere beneath the surface of who we really are, a personal almost closeted conversation with ourselves, a searching to better understand the person within, and the desires that drive us. Perhaps also for Carol it was a need to explore other areas of a life in question; to know her inner self and to reach a place where she could take such a challenge without it hurting. But there were no rules to follow; no guidelines to help through the emotions that must have been at times confused and desperate. The reality was, she needed to feel and know a special affection, a closeness and an intimacy she could trust. Something she could hold on to. She had struggled to find both meaning and purpose in her young life. This choice then, and the attraction it held for her would be a whole new experience with a different set of parameters than she was used to. No doubt, in the quiet hours of the night she would find herself the victim of unexpected trepidation and anxiety brought-on by thoughts of an unknown venture into a totally different world. Still, she felt driven to try.

Although not often realized - and frequently misunderstood, such an attraction is not as unusual as it may seem at first glance. Carol's new quest is best seen through the lens of not only her gender, but also the stresses and pressures that consumed her over a long period of time. Regardless, lesbian experiences are not necessarily a question of preference of one gender over another. It's to some extent, and in some circumstances better explained when we become aware of the natural fluidity of a woman's sexuality. Women biologically or psychologically have at times a greater tendency, or willingness to explore a bi-sexual experience than most men do. The paradigms of 'normal' relationships are not necessarily as fixed as many believe, and other occasional affairs of the heart or mind can sometimes take their place, at least for a while. And just maybe it's a good time to glance at a few of those realities when thinking of one woman being attracted to another.

In Carol's case, she had known frequent severe physical and emotional abuse with some men. It encouraged a lack of trust that left her always feeling she couldn't be herself; unable to embrace the comfort and emotional security she needed. There was a deep thirst for a meaningful connection with someone special that couldn't be quenched in any traditional way. She had lived through a kaleidoscope of numerous and varied psychological provocations; emotional upheavals and endless let-downs with potential partners. She had searched her dreams for a love that was full of all she could have imagined. Yet they remained for the most part, a dream. Now, all she wanted in her private life was a love without the reek of a man's lust, where the coming chapters of life would hold a contentment and an acceptance she could call her own. She wanted to feel whole. Complete.

Relationships with another woman, while not perhaps perfect, rarely experience the sort of negative behavior she had known in the past, although it remained a possibility. But the experience could be expressed differently through the unique feminine alliance. As a consequence, an individual can feel relatively 'safe' in that sense, but still carry the feelings from unhappy and unfruitful associations. Sometimes the thoughts leave one tending to accept the love we think we deserve. Still, Carol carried with her through the years a strong feeling of guilt and justified anger for in truth she had been exploited and used. But the comfort she perceived or anticipated through her liaison with another woman represented a new possibility as she gave way to her deepest emotions and their intrinsic vulnerability.

Considering the insecurity and questions felt through such a journey, 'experimenting' to find gratification on many levels might provide for some women a sense of comfort. They may well feel better understood for one thing. Also, by their very nature, unlike men, they're encouraged or programed to be friendly and open with each-other. That alone can produce a feeling of greater affinity and trust; a particular closeness and availability. A certain familiarity can grow very quickly when people lay-open their feelings and needs, producing thoughts of a refreshing sense of intimacy if a woman's 'traditional' love life is in difficulty or threatened.

Acceptance, respect and love itself is paramount in the search for that ultimate level of companionship. And in fact, these are the needs of every single human being on the planet.

But one of the most desperate of all is that of complete emotional approbation; the celebration of belonging, where we can safely surrender our vulnerabilities and affection to another. We will go to extremes to achieve this end in our search for a partner. These are paradigms that at first may appear confusing and at times even contradictory. But one has to open the mind to a woman's particular, peculiar and unique hunger. She needs to be with a partner who exhibits a strong and independent emotional integrity where she sees strength and feels secure in her identity. She needs the freedom to indulge in her own humanity and sexuality as something that is 'sine qua non' - that essential indispensable ingredient that for her, cements a relationship. Regardless, the fact remains that a high percentage of heterosexual women have felt at one time or another a strong attraction toward another woman at some time in their lives. But of those involved in a close relationship, only a little over 12% have actually experienced full intimacy.

During this time in Carol's journey drinking took-on an even more important role than before. The dependency seemed even greater and it had become totally out of control; heavy and sustained because of the immense reliance she had on it, and what it appeared to do for her. In the darkest hours and through every conceivable challenge she needed more to satisfy her needs; to allow some reprieve and taste even a moment of comfort or peace. It was the only thing that kept her going; the only thing that helped her cope with the daily pressures she was under. Her personal life was in question, and threatened to reach a crisis point before much longer.

Her life in the office and as manager was extraordinarily stressful and demanding, both in time and psychologically. And then there was the coming home to uncertainty; to questions and even guilt, feeling unsure of her next step but wanting with every ounce of her strength to have things work and make sense. She wanted more than life itself to know the bond and meaning of being truly loved for who she was; to be able to turn with confidence from the gnawing fear of the unknown and the possibility of loss. The thoughts and insecurities that would stay with her from the life she knew just a handful of years before were impossible to deal with; overwhelming and debilitating. Again a drink might ease the fear, if only for the night, and help take away the inhibitions to circumstances that might present themselves over the hours. For many of us it's simply called 'survival'.

There is however yet another particularly dark side to the problem of drinking and to the life of someone addicted. It places them at serious risk for so many adverse consequences, and impacts dramatically on their personal life in ways often not recognized. Drinking as a lifestyle results in certain self-defeating behaviors as a way of coping with stress. And in relationships, not just within a marriage but also amongst others, 'intimacy' is often one of its first casualties. With trust taken away, and filled with self-doubt, the inability to relate as they should takes a heavy toll on mutuality and closeness within a relationship, and often a partner may pull-back emotionally as a way of protecting themselves. It often results in a broken bond between partners if not caught in time. In effect, 'drink' becomes that other 'person' in their lives, leaving them with little time for others, no matter how close they may have been in their togetherness. It is devastating, and struggling with it alone is overwhelming. But sometimes there is an actual fear of true intimacy or closeness because of the possibility of failing, resulting in fear itself driving a person away from ever finding it. To the surprise of some, real intimacy affects even more than the obvious connection to another and the corresponding comfort they experience. Psychologically, it also has an effect on our spiritual needs for it's a major component in our spiritual walk. And particularly, the victims of alcohol abuse often feel closed-off from others - and even from God. The struggle can truly be monumental.

The trails of bottles were everywhere at this time of her life, and always hidden out of necessity in closets or under stairs, and at work in drawers or cabinets as was convenient. She knew of the dangers. She knew of the stigma of getting caught. The embarrassment. The humiliation. The loss of trust and disrespect. It was socially all so conveniently explained and outlined for the abuser. But what wasn't so easily explained was the question of WHY? And in a sense that is one of the greatest tragedies of all. The fact was, Carol, like so many others who had taken to drinking and who had become, descriptively an alcoholic, were sadly not understanding nor aware of the reality of their vulnerability. But then how could they, given what they were facing, and their earlier preparations (or lack-of) for dealing with the curves Life often throws at us. Of course they were probably quite unable to reach for the resources available. Or to trust them as they experienced the horrors; the psychological and emotional pain of their walk. They were and are most often, simply the victims of a situation or set of circumstances they had no control over. The fact was, it had become a very serious problem for Carol, already impacting heavily on every area of her life.

Those of us under duress, and frequently drinking excessively are very often responding to early childhood experiences, and even earlier learned drinking habits if they started while still young. Many, burdened with such a problem knew difficulties in infancy as families struggled with their own trauma and misfortune - and even with the heavy use of alcohol around the house. And if the stresses are considerable through infancy and adolescence, the prolonged struggles they experience can permanently change the hormonal stress response, effecting how they later respond and react to new challenges as they grow older. Many though, through learned behavior or genetic expression will turn to the bottle when the pressures of life become overwhelming. And that is the ultimate tragedy with this disease.

It's interesting to note that for a woman, alcohol has even added effects for they don't process it as efficiently as men do. Generally they absorb more of it, and because of the concentration, it takes longer to process. Another way of looking at it is to say that even when drinking the same amount, they will have higher levels of alcohol in their blood than a man would. Also the actual effects of the liquor are much more immediate and last longer. Some of the reasons are obvious, such as on average a woman weighs less than a man. Women also have less water in their bodies - and it's in the body water that alcohol disperses more readily. Briefly then, a woman's brain, and even other organs tend to be significantly more vulnerable to drinking, and the effects can be more profound overall. So, in some ways, she faces greater challenges when alcohol becomes a part of her life. She responds differently, or certainly can. And almost half of females who were introduced to drinking before the age of fifteen would become alcohol dependent at some point in their lives - especially in the presence of certain stresses.

As it was, Carol's new venture into the previously unknown world of relationships with others of her gender was shortlived, and she never was able to put aside nor forget the ache she held for the union of souls; for that special person who would accept her, love her and fill the needs that gripped the heart of this child of God. Surely there had to be a virtual soul mate somewhere in this world she could happily connect with.

With the passing of time, and no-doubt noticing her friends and colleagues moving-on with their own relationships, she succumbed to the pressures she felt and decided to place an add in an on-line singles column. The results were momentous in their own way. Yet not nearly as positive as she had hoped. For such an attractive young woman, the move brought endless dates and opportunities. But the men she met seemed for the most part as lost and as mixed-up as she herself had felt for such a long time. It was not the least bit encouraging. Many were dysfunctional and confused with their own lives, looking hopefully to connect as best they could wherever they may be accepted while they struggled to have their own needs filled. In them she found no sense of happiness or joy; no comfort to sustain the hope she held for a truly successful and meaningful relationship. It left her feeling even more desperately alone in some strange way, and by the time she met Mike she was about to give-up.

They stayed together for some time, revolving around each-other's lives and tolerating each-other's addictions; his to drugs and the alcohol for Carol. These were stressful times; difficult emotionally, but given their own unique histories and human desires, they took the big step of getting married. It wasn't at all evident in the beginning, but Mike had a serious issue with control, and after a while his motives became clear to his relatively new wife. He was the boss. In control. And it would be in her best interest to listen to his lead and tow the line. But she had long tired of abuse by others; the demands of men who pressed upon her their practical need and craving for satisfaction. She had had enough and refused to take it, unlike the girl of earlier years. Now nothing seemed to work which might save them as a couple. Sides were taken and the relationship became so fragmented there was no reason to continue. She soon filed for divorce, and although the circumstances were difficult and awkward, it finally went though and she was free.

The action must have left her feeling she was back in control to some extent. She had made a wise choice, and acted on the decision to end the suffering she experienced with this man. It was a good move. Positive. And full of hope in one sense, although she would continue to feel the apparent loss or failure of another close connection. But things could only improve after this fragile relationship came to an end.

Chapter Twelve

ALL FOR THE LOVE OF YOU

WHEN A RELATIONSHIP COMES TO AN END, no matter whose fault floats to the surface or the freedom it may bring, there is most often a considerable psychological distress to deal with. Even self-doubt. Thoughts will naturally take turns thinking back on the experiences shared and the good times; the times when you felt really nothing could come between you. Often the pain felt after a breakup is severe and can in fact manifest itself much like a physical pain. Thoughts can become obsessive and deeply worrisome while reflecting on how everything could have fallen apart after the earlier passion of being with that special person. Feelings will find themselves searching for what really did go wrong, and asking could it have worked if it had been approached differently. Regardless, for Carol a self-compassion was growing as she realized the difficult position she had been in, and the futility of a satisfying and fulfilling future with this partner. It was over, and the aggression she had witnessed toward the end had triggered her decision to move-on. It wouldn't be long before she would become fully aware of that reality. She really was free to get-on with the rest of her life, with new dreams and expectations - and that ever-present sense of hope she needed to hold-on to.

It wasn't long before Carol found herself invited to a friend's wedding. The unusual thing about it was this romantic event was to be held on a beach in South Western Ontario. Of course she was eager to go and be a part of it. But perhaps the last thing she could have expected was meeting Dave; a handsome man, fun-loving and down to earth. From the start they appeared to have a lot in common and they could relax around each-other; enjoy each-other's company and feel a sense of belonging even at this early stage. There was a definite electricity between them and an understanding which encouraged a particular level of comfort from the very beginning. Even the private thoughts of a future together; growing together and sharing dreams were positive and hopeful. The core of this relationship seemed different; constructive and waiting only for direction. Now all Carol needed at this point was to learn to trust. But that would not be easy after the experiences she'd had with partners. Still, she could already feel the comfort of what some have called one of the most wonderful gifts of all; to be understood. It was a particularly promising experience, and gave the spark of something she had waited so very long for. As the romance blossomed into one of steady dating and a closeness, it was all looking good. In the deepest part of who she was as a woman, she felt intuitively this was the man she had been waiting for. Her life was beginning to change, and began to head in a direction she had hoped for. At last there seemed a special purpose to work toward. Perhaps a door was opening to a new life where she would come to know joy and happiness, and that precious feeling of security and love. Perhaps she could at last think of putting down roots from which to grow. She found moments to reflect on the past exploits and misadventures; thought of what she had learned from each painful pilgrimage. But of those early beginnings and the guilt that still haunted her, she would in time come to understand another truth about the human condition - that at some level of our journey, as Simone Weil once said, the sins we accept - all sins in fact are in the end, but a desperate excuse to fill a void in our lives. And so we struggle-on.

More than ever before, things were on track for Carol. She was happy with how the relationship was unfolding, and while for some time they were living in different cities, they would arrange to meet out of town often mid-week to be to-gether and enjoy each-other's company. She was basking in a happiness she had never known before and was beginning to trust again. In Dave she had found a man who wanted to be involved with her; wanted to be close while showing interest and concern for her welfare and health. They pulled togeth-er to make it into a lasting affair where they could relax, with a feeling of confidence that they could make it work. Like all relationships, there were times when they would struggle with their own needs, and with the pressures to meet those of their partner. But they would usually prevail and climb-up to the next level where they could move-on. It was all so encouraging.

In time of course the moment came when they realized they must make some decisions as to whether they should commit to becoming even closer - and to making their time together easier. The stress of the long-distant communication was getting to them and causing concern for both. It had become too much, with the demands on time; the problems that would arise as the months went by.

The situation was bringing pressures they didn't need at this critical time in their lives, and choices had to be made. If this was going to work at all, one of them had to move. With Carol's career moving ahead in such a positive way, they decided it would be best for Dave to move the seventy five miles into the city where she was living.

Searching the town for living opportunities, they settled on buying a house together close to the downtown and not far from her place of work. It looked ideal from the beginning. In part because of the time committed to being together, and working as a team, the relationship grew in strength, enriched by all the good things they could offer each-other. They were both sincere, honest people who wanted to reach their dream of a trusting and comfortable rapport where the future offered the hope of fulfillment and total commitment to each-other in a solid relationship. Already their level of communication was good and they would share their personal lives constructively and with deep affection. She felt strengthened and loved really for the first time in her life. This clearly was the real thing. How different things seemed from the days when she had been so abused by her partners. Now she was not fearful. Rather she loved this man passionately and trusted him such that over time they grew closer and experienced a level of devotion and care she could never have imagined possible.

The world changes color and flavor when two people in love begin their new lives together. It all becomes more intense and exciting, with so much to look forward to when the future is faced as a couple. And that's how it should be. Naturally, with past experiences and related memories there is always a level of caution. And it was no different with Carol and Dave. While both recognized the qualities they saw in each-other, becoming increasingly aware of how special their relationship was, things would progress at a pace that was comfortable for them individually. And it was worth all they could give, and more. Together they worked hard at keeping it focused and fulfilling, and as a team put their shoulders to the wheel to strengthen each-other and give the support and trust each had been hoping for. Now the days were bright with hope and a growing satisfaction for how their lives were unfolding. And the more they would come to know each-other, the stronger their feeling and ties of commitment. It had over a short period of time developed into a deeply meaningful relationship.

Of course, starting a new life together comes with its own challenges which can be difficult for both parties. Getting to really know each-other under these different and demanding circumstances is very hard. How much should one give? How might my partner respond if he or she knows how I feel about this or that. Then there's the sharing and coming to understand each-other's beliefs and values. And often after only a little while, the worry over trust in all these areas can become a problem.

There are issues of intimacy and needs; likes and dislikes; unexpected perspectives and the stresses of work. Housework and basic chores and simply feeling respected and appreciated. There can be problems with other family members with their own thoughts and expectations. We all come with our own baggage; habits left-over from our first families and growing-up. And habits are hard to break. Even the question of who will lead can become problematic. Most of us want to live on equal terms and be treated that way. But often things and attitudes can be cultural and almost inbred. It all takes time. There's often the problem from the beginning with finances and sharing, sometimes leaving one feeling they are putting in more than their share. Money is a huge issue for couples, often throughout their marriage. And it becomes a balancing act that all too often tends to go one way. And when that happens, we become resentful and even bitter. Right or wrong, it's still a reality. Ideally when that is the case, selective counseling can help put things back into perspective. But it takes two to make it work. And that's where honesty and trust really come into the picture.

They would live together for a number of years before the decision to marry made itself known with Dave's unexpected proposal, and she was happy to accept. Things had been working so well for them, first in their togetherness as a couple, but also in their lives in the work-place. Dave had an excellent job that was rewarding in itself as well as financially. And Carol had already been climbing the corporate ladder and was a senior manager in her own right. The compensation was even more than she could have imagined, and together they faced a future with increasing confidence with respect to security over the long term. Life, and even married life at last was good. More than likely, in the quiet moments that settle on us through the day, she must have thought back to those times with Derrick as well as others. She would have reflected on her feelings as a young girl, and then as a woman without influence or power; without the full respect of her peers. In the minutes pressed behind a humbling smile, she may have dwelt on her early vulnerability, and a certain hopelessness when she was at the mercy of others. We can only marvel at how lives can change direction and head down paths we could never have even imagined in our youth. And for Carol, the best was yet to come. But it would take time, and some challenging and even horrifying experiences.

Over a very few short years she had become a woman of influence and power; a woman who received the respect of others. And it felt good. She had earned her place in the sun, and the rewards it gave; the comfort she felt from what she had achieved. Over the months and even the early years together, and for reasons described in Chapter One, she would commit more and more time to her job, bringing work home to carry her into the night with ever-increasing demands. But there was progress along with the late hours she gave, yet it began to consume her time and energy in many areas of her life. In one sense it was perfect, filling thoughts with the responsibilities she faced every day, while allowing her to deal with the occasional challenges in her marriage. It wasn't that the love for each-other had failed. Not at all. But it was in some ways scattered and unfocused; diffused through a kaleidoscope of seasons, struggles and anxious anticipation. As a result of these pressures, she began to believe, once again she couldn't really trust anyone - not even her husband as far as her emotional needs were concerned. Perhaps it's better explained as the growing absence of a close affection, and a feeling of loss to the sense of belonging.

There's little doubt in some ways she didn't even believe herself to be 'loveable'. But whatever the cause, sadly the results left her feeling abandoned emotionally; disconnected from what she really wanted from life; insecure even in whatever love was left. Yet she tried to meet the demands of her husband in every imaginable way, and believed she did. But gnawing insidious suspicions brought her to re-think opportunities that over time presented themselves again and again. There were always the "what if 's" and thoughts of added security with others stolen from the moments she wanted desperately to give to her husband. But at times it was difficult, and the future, frightening. Often there would be a fear or even a disruption in intimacy - and a longing to find it 'somewhere' perhaps with 'someone' if things didn't work-out as they should.

Tragically, such feelings describe a picture of a child who had been sexually abused. Not only their innocence, but also their trust is taken away, along with any self-esteem and they may experience all kinds of dysfunctional relationships often beginning in adolescence with promiscuous behavior that in the end is hopelessly self-defeating. In marriage, it's not unusual for a female victim of early abuse to question the nature and needs of her husband for sometimes he may appear to her as having certain characteristics of her offender. Perhaps she 'sees' his motives as she eventually came to see the motives of the man who used her as a young girl. Could her husband be doing the very same thing? Might he too be only using her for his own gratification? It's not unusual then for a woman to respond even in subtle ways to her husband much as she had to her offender all those years ago. Unknown to the victim, even in adulthood, a child can in fact over time internalize the 'messages' she came to see from her abuser. Consequently, any sexual or emotional seduction from even an adult partner may trigger under some circumstances a familiar response - unconsciously 'connected' to situations around her first abusive experience. It is complicated and subtle. Even confusing. But when a young woman, after suffering the trauma of abuse with no-one to stand by her, is committed to a relationship - there are fears attached; the origins of which she may never be fully aware of. In the end, it led her into new circumstances in an attempt to keep the dream alive - and to simply survive the only way she knew how.

So, things happened and were experienced only out of the desperate needs experienced as a young girl in a faraway town a long way away. Things happened because of the insecurities she knew all too well. She must give all: everything to gain the love of another. She herself could never be enough; never be sufficient to hold the affection of this man unless she could give even more of herself. But the ground she was on soon became shaky as a result of the activities planned in the first place to make their relationship even stronger. And she found herself spinning wildly in a whirlpool of doubt, fear and uncertainty. Where would this all end?

Left confused and hurting, uncertain of her personal life for the future and overworked with her job, she was vulnerable and afraid. And no matter the thoughts the reader may entertain, each of us play the game of life only with the cards we were dealt with. It's as simple as that. And no matter how we might try, we are not given a second hand. But there is hope. For while the cards may not change, their values certainly can, and even how they are played. And this is what happened to Carol over the years. The experiences described in the earlier chapters, and the eventual meeting with Landon resulted from the very set of circumstances outlined over these pages. In fact, it was this sheer desperation that drove a confused young woman on an adventure into the sun-kissed seas of the Caribbean to take that emotional detour into the arms of another man, and interestingly into another experience that would change her life forever.

Chapter Thirteen

TELL ME WHERE GOD IS

TIME HAS ITS OWN WAY OF MOVING-ON. And for Carol and Dave, life followed an almost predictable path over the months following her return from the affair with Landon. But much had been learned through the experience. And so many of the events that unfolded over those years have already been described through Carol's determination to have her story told. And it's courageous of her to allow this glimpse into a very personal experience that has in the end demanded a voice of its own.

Looking back to that long painful night at the retreat, where after the call from her husband she fell to her knees in prayer, there was a long period of silence before receiving any answer to her dilemma. There was also the question of God and His reality lurking somewhere in the heart, but it was illusive and vague, moving in and out of focus in an unashamed and confused uncertainty. But she had returned home with a profound sense of relief, finding Dave to be none the wiser to what had transpired over that time. Still, she was badly shaken, fully realizing how close she had come to losing all she held dear; the husband she really did love when all the hungers and thirsts for survival and self-preservation could be put aside.

Regardless, even given the issues and pressures; the demands that percolated into their daily life, they soon fell into step again with each-other. There would be a few changes to a style that had become familiar to them, accepting the pace and flavor with all its complications and challenges. Still insecure, and searching, at least for Carol for that all illusive sense of satisfaction, they took most things in stride, getting-on with their lives at home as well as in the workplace. In fact it was there she made the acquaintance of a gentleman who'd been attending his own church in the east end of the city. At times he would spend moments talking with her and even leaving tracts in the hope they would be read. And they were. Over a while she would think about attending church - but which one? Anyway, surely there was perhaps no real hurry, and that decision or choice could wait a while longer.

Many months slipped by before accepting the invitation from her colleague to worship in the house of God, and she continued to drink heavily after slipping again into that earlier life-style. Even then, she could see clearly the effects it was having on her life. No matter what she involved herself in, there was no escaping the sense of hopelessness that settled over her once more, pervading her life and poking it's cold hand into every corner of her being. It haunted her; almost possessed her through her waking hours until her drinking became even more excessive; guarded and secret in the hope that her husband would not realize how serious it had become. She knew from earlier comments; his very nature and his limits, that if there was even a hint of betrayal by her, or deceit, he would pack his things and leave. His father had been the very same way and she knew he meant it. She had to be careful; play everything just right to avoid any suspicion. But it was difficult - and becoming more so as one day moved into another.

Along with other things she was involved with during this hectic time, and while still working in her management position, she was given an opportunity to work for a cosmetics company - the Mary Kay Corporation. It was something she could never have imagined herself doing; not being particularly comfortable nor even interested in sales. But it was a product she had used herself for some time, and the thought came to her that she could influence the lives of other young women by promoting and encouraging the use of their product. On top of that, it was an interesting and exciting challenge and she decided to take advantage of it.

The whole approach of the company jumped out at you once you had made its acquaintance. It was bold. Even brash perhaps in the world of inter-personal commerce. The founder of the company, Mary Kay Ash was truly an original entrepreneur and philanthropist, starting her business from a small store in Dallas Texas more than fifty years ago. Like Martin Luther King she had a dream, and her dream basically was to simply inspire women with the intent on transforming their lives and helping them achieve success in both their personal and professional lives. The focus would be on them feeling and looking their best while making their mark at home and in the work-place. She held a passion for beautifying lives and helping women achieve the successes they were capable of.

Consequently, It wasn't long before Carol started working part-time, selling cosmetics of every kind and having her own needs in that area met, and at a significant discount, which was a real incentive. On top of that, she found the Mary Kay company to be most unusual in another way; they believed and taught that even in industry, God comes first, the family second, and the career third. It was for her at that time a unique perspective, and it was a story also shared with each and every one of her clients. It did in fact teach a lesson in values and prioritized the focus each consultant should have when dealing with the public.

In many ways it proved a fascinating venture, so much so that for a while she considered leaving her blue-ribbon job and making it her career choice. It had already given her considerable experience with the public and extra money to spend. It also was a significant help in dealing with feelings of an innate shyness she always had since childhood. In fact it gave her an even greater sense of being in control - not only from a business perspective, but also in her private life that was still suffering. In a way it was an adventure into a whole new area of merchandising where she could put her already excellent business skills to good use and develop a new level of confidence. And together, this stood to influence every other area of her life.

For the next while she pursued her goals, attending meetings and seminars and serving her clientele in every possible way. She was eager; excited at the possibilities her hard work could bring. There was planning to be addressed; prioritizing and organizing the sometimes confusing details of even a small business venture, but by her very nature she was superb at the challenges she faced. She enjoyed it, and I suspect, at first perhaps much to her surprise. The experience was satisfying as well as being very positive, and it filled a need she had when other thoughts would consume her. She continued to work at it for a considerable time, still with the thought in back on her mind that this in fact may well be the career she was best suited for. But the question would come-up as to how she could possibly know for sure. The business venture offered much - but so did the steady work in management, with all its perks and offers of a satisfying pension by the age of 55. There was a lot to consider before making a choice. As it was, she didn't have long to wait to find her answer.

Chapter Fourteen

THE HOUSE OF GOD

CAROL HAD BEEN THINKING OF CHURCH. SHE had even considered the large and stately United Church which was not far from where she worked. In her day job she would often think on it. But she was still undecided. There was much going-on in her life, and it wasn't at this time anyway a top priority given her busy schedule and the demands on her which seemed to grow exponentially as the days slipped into weeks. But over the coming months, and with thoughts of it stirring in her mind, she made the decision one day to attend church the following Sunday. She decided it would be the one encouraged by her friend and co-worker, and as it happened, it was the one closest to her home just east of the city limits. At least the location was ideal and could be reached in short order. Perhaps in some way, the very convenience of it helped her make that final decision; a decision that was to be another major step into the world - and yet one that would in so many ways help her step out of it and into a new life. But still, the results of one's actions may take time to become apparent, even after careful thought. Yet what was about to happen was something she could never have expected nor ever imagined possible.

When that unforgettable Sunday arrived, she left her house and climbed into her car, driving perhaps more slowly than usual, finding the building without too much difficulty. A second glance and she turned into the parking-lot perhaps with a feeling of uncertainty. Possibly with a degree of anxiety as to what she might find. But this was her choice. Her decision. It was in fact the one thing she was now determined to do. After only a limited pause; a few breaths and a controlled excitement, she stepped out of the car and headed for the front door of the church. Looking up, she found herself climbing the eight steps leading up to the Pentecostal Church which was nestled in the midst of an older residential neighborhood in the east end of the city.

There was no hesitation as she pulled on the doors to the lobby, then a second set, to find herself walking into the sanctuary of the church that seemed to have been waiting for her. She was immediately filled with an emotion she had never experienced before. Being early, there were not too many people about. But it seemed as if she was entering another world; a place in many ways so foreign to her. Still, she was gripped with a certain reassurance of peace and a presence she would never forget - nor get away from again. She noticed the large cross mounted on the wall behind the platform where the morning sermon would be given, and glanced at the wooden pews that lined each side, standing like sentinels from another time and place. Walking slowly toward the front, she noticed a picture that had been taped to the front of the pulpit just a few feet away. It was of a woman kneeling in prayer, with the words, "Ladies of

Zion" printed boldly beneath, and her attention would return to that image again and again over the coming hour. Although not knowing at the time what it meant, she was taken by the image of the woman in prayer, and was overwhelmed with the thought and memory of that moment back at the retreat those months ago - of herself kneeling in prayer and desperation as she asked for help, pleading to God for His intervention and deliverance from the emotional pain she was suffering, and from a life that had left her shaken and lost.

Through a series of events over the years, and the decisions she had made with little or no support or guidance, she had disconnected from the things she had loved the most and dreamed-of. Now, so many emotions would flood over her, and with the service still minutes away from beginning, tears, hot tears fell onto her face as if cleansing her very heart of the hurt and anguish she had lived through over the years. And so she sat in the quiet of the sanctuary letting the feelings flood over her; the healing she was already beginning to feel. With her eyes still filled, she became strangely aware of a new awareness. She was 'home'. It was to be a prophetic moment in her life.

As the minutes unfolded, people drifted into their places and seats; some men to the platform where they settled into the chairs lined-up in preparation for the morning service. Soon ladies joined them at the organ and piano off to the left, and to the right she could see the drums waiting their turn to be included, and she remembered thinking how strange it was - the thought of drums in a church. But the stillness was about to be broken in a most wonderful way. Within moments the church came to life with words of welcome and warmth, along with the carefully planned music and song. It was a beautiful setting for this first visit to a place that over the years would become so very familiar, and she immediately felt welcomed; accepted and acknowledged in this totally new setting. As it happened, the ladies prayer group had in fact been praying for her for some time, prompted no doubt by her colleague who had approached her much earlier about his church.

That morning she felt the overpowering presence, known surely in Heaven itself as her prayers began to be answered, along with the first one spoken on her knees while facing the loss of all that was dear to her; the night when she cried-out to God. As she sat in the pew alone with her thoughts, the worship service continued to lift her through the words and hymns that seemed to penetrate every fibre of her being. It has been said that tears are the prayers of a broken spirit, and now they flowed freely as she wept, her heart now open to this new experience of feeling the acceptance of God. She couldn't escape the image of the woman on her knees, and gave-in to the feelings that swept over her. And the cosmetics she had used and sold now ran in streaks down her face, for nothing in creation could stop the weeping. But it was a cleansing outpouring of her very soul as perhaps for the very first time she felt her mind opening to the sermon; the message and to the presence she was feeling through it all. She listened intently, absorbed by the ambience of her surroundings; the complexion of this special place. By the end of the service she received such a conviction after re-living her life; an exposed life now washed by His promise and her own endless tears that reached into her being with forgiveness and hope. Finally there was an alter call, where those gathered were invited to the front to worship openly and freely before the cross. Time had moved so quickly since first walking through those doors, and she found herself looking around, feeling the pulse of the congregation. She noticed the people getting-up from their seats and walking toward the front. Some knelt while others stood with hands raised in worship; heads sometimes tilted as they reached-out for the presence of God each in his own way. She was lifted by the moment and the feelings that had moved through her, and stood to join them; to throw herself at His feet. A presence flowed through her as if a culmination to the prayer she had prayed in the middle of her pain some time before. She reached the alter and fell to her knees, her soul still sobbing in the ultimate comforting company of The Lord. She had never known such emotional power and its need to express all that had been on her heart. And she not only embraced the ubiquity of the moment; the certainty of His reality and power, but felt the embrace of His love, majesty and authority within and surrounding her. She felt herself gripped by His gentle hand as she was carried into the fold; a once lost sheep looking into the face of her shepherd.

That first experience at church was immediately followed by her pastor approaching her before she left, to introduce himself and to ask of her visit. While in her heart she already had the right way in mind, she blurted-out her need to be baptized. In his wisdom he slowed the pace and asked if she really knew the reason for such a serious commitment. She didn't, feeling that was all she must do to be saved. But he explained in a tone of infinite kindness and compassion that there was more she must understand. Much more she needed to be ready for. And to prepare for.

And baptism in her church meant a complete immersion into the baptismal tank. Although it is of course a necessary step in the process of Salvation, it makes public the profession of Faith and Obedience to the command of Jesus. There must be full repentance of sin for the candidate to be baptized in the name of Jesus Christ. And it's essential Scripture is understood and accepted by all those taking this path into a life with Christ.

It was yet another powerful moment, and after a brief talk, it was suggested she engage in a Bible Study before even considering the thought of baptism. She was anxious to do anything necessary to be saved and to know the love of Jesus. And it wasn't long before it was arranged, with plans to meet weekly with the pastor and his wife. Instead of it being held at her house, she had declined the offer only because of a concern for her husband's perspective as he'd often shown distrust and frustration at any religious group stopping by. Consequently it was decided to hold the sessions in the church office where she could fully involve herself and invest her increasing thirst for knowledge in that safe and private environment. She felt comfortable there, and free to involve herself completely in the program. The material covered, along with various CD's given by the same colleague who had invited her to church began to have an enormous influence in her life.

While she still listened to the music of the world; perhaps even pieces she had grown-up with over the years, the material began to impact her deeply, displacing to a large extent those other daily needs and even patterns of thought and behavior. She was excited at the changes she felt, and the involvement with church gave her a new hope to go-on.

It seemed that finally a new peace was settling about her, and everyday things and experiences began to take-on a new meaning. There was purpose to her life now. And it gave her the confidence to face the challenges with renewed energy. She even contemplated the possibility and hope of introducing her husband to a special sense of well-being she was becoming more and more familiar with. But even then she knew that would take time. Now though, for the first time in her adult life, and in her new and encouraging surroundings she began to feel a freedom and the liberty to fully express her love for Jesus; the Lord who had become at last her precious saviour. After so many years of despair and pain, she was finally able to put her past life behind her to move-on. The only way now was forward, with thoughts of a future that was bright with hope and encouragement.

Chapter Fifteen

THE STRENGTH TO FORGIVE

OVER THE COMING MONTHS THERE WOULD BE much for her to adjust to after this beginning with her new-found faith. Thoughts and even attitudes began to reconfigure, along with the language she was naturally so familiar with. Words were more carefully chosen, and moments of frustration were not verbalized in the old way. Missing were the selected comments or cliche's that would have been used freely and often in her everyday interactions with others, and she noticed greater attention being paid to correct any accidental slip of the tongue. But Life would go-on and changes made that would in the end impact all those around her. She began to notice friends who had shared a particular style of living were dropping away as they saw the changes in her life and attitude and her lack of interest in the things they did together. And the earlier recreational or 'social' activity that had been introduced into her marriage as an attempt to infuse a passion and meaning into their personal lives had in fact seen its last days. It had started essentially as a way of drawing them closer emotionally as well as physically, but she had come to see the damage it was doing to them as a couple. The loss of trust of each-other. Doubts and infidelity. There were frequent feelings of jealousy that would eat away at her, and misdirected desires that left her in the end, fearful and anxious; unsafe and disconnected from the man she loved.

While Carol was noticing dramatic changes already in her walk with God, Dave, while not fully understanding what was really happening to his wife never questioned nor held her back from pursuing the new goal she had set for herself. Still, in the darker moments of her days she continued to struggle with alcohol, trying to deal with its influence which had been established so very long ago. It was quite simply a part of her life; of who she was, and one she felt helped her in its own bizarre way through many difficulties at home and in the workplace. It provided a relief from the struggles she still found herself in at times. And out of desperation she would reach for a drink to calm the moments that seemed to gang-up on her; the pressures of daily life that were at times impossible to deal with, leaving her feeling overwhelmed and powerless. Now the need was as strong as ever and she drank whenever she could to help cope with all the demands she was facing. No matter how she handled it, its use was concealed from her husband.

Regardless, with great determination she continued with church which by now had become an essential and necessary part of her life. She looked forward to it, attending not only the Sunday morning services, but also the one offered in the evening. Soon she was also making time for the Bible Study sessions held on a weekly basis every Tuesday night. It was meeting her needs spiritually, and she was being fed in other ways; ways that not only enriched her new walk with God, but that also brought a growing peace into her life. Attending to church was the one thing she felt she could trust, believe in and depend on; an environment she felt safe in. It gave her comfort and promised hope if she stayed with the journey. And that she was determined to do. At every opportunity she would take her worries and her fears to the alter - at the feet of Christ, seeking divine intervention from the Lord, and praying for the peace she knew was there once she had shown her obedience to Him. The hours spent in the pew were not always easy by any means. The messages with every service painfully exposed a past sinful life, with characteristics that would in the end lead to her very destruction unless they were stopped. That was what all this was about. It was about the need to find control and stability in her life; to find the tranquility she needed to feel in her heart. She needed to know in the very center of her being that she was 'safe' and the future blessed with promises and dreams. She needed perhaps above all, to know she was truly loved for who she was; a young woman taking her first steps into a new life, hopefully handin-hand with her partner. One surely couldn't ask for more. Even with the positive changes of those first few months attending church, and with determination and resolve, there were issues she still faced seemingly alone. One of the key tenets of her faith revolved around the need to forgive. And that she realized was something she needed to do for the man who had seduced and taken advantage of her as a young teenage girl. In fact it was essential for her to move on. It wasn't only a good idea - it was a necessary move on a conscious level, and it had to be exercised. But it was hard. Difficult. Seemingly impossible at some level. Yet it had to be done. And soon. It was also essential she forgave not only the man, but also herself. Unless that was realized and accepted in the very core of her being, the future lay fallow and uncertain, empty in some strange way. But perhaps even before herself, she needed to release him with a forgiveness that came from the heart.

Scripture is clear in saying if we cannot forgive those who have transgressed against us, then God will not forgive us our own morally delinquent choices; our mistakes and hurtful actions. She had to make that decision and then act on it as soon as she was able. But it was something she would struggle with for some time. When seeking true forgiveness, just how far can we, or should we go? And should it be at the cost to others? She sought counsel from the pastor whom she trusted above anyone, and he believed it wise under the circumstances to hold back the truth from the related parties. He recommended not divulging the event for fear of the damage it could do to others. But Carol still needed to forgive the man.

The tension from it all was unbearably painful and traumatic. And complicated in the extreme. And there was only so much she felt she could share with her husband at this point in their relationship. There were quite simply things he still wasn't fully aware of, and she lived continuously in the fear of his finding-out and possibly leaving. The circumstances were heavy and bewildering, and difficult to deal with. There was still so much at stake on an everyday level, with memories and emotions seemingly hiding around each corner waiting for their opportunity to leap back into her life. And work was also making ever-increasing demands on her. But as much as her life was already changing, there were lots to be anxious about and fearful of. She had to be careful and cautious.

The seriousness of the situation she was facing was all too evident, and it's understandable how this new child of God would have been driven to seek Him in those desperate moments just months before. While the immediacy may have eased, the problems still raised their power over her peace with the fear they left in her heart. But she had made those first steps into a new life with new expectations and values; with refreshed determination to make things 'right' and to bring new meaning and purpose to her life. It was bold and magnificent. Though surely at that moment in time she never would have recognized the courage she had shown. And through this window we see the true personality and character of this young woman who had struggled over the years to find the happiness she truly deserved; that we all deserve - and the passion she had shown not only to change the direction of her Life, but to make amends and come to terms with the past. It was a movement of heroic proportions and extraordinary consequences. And she would make the effort this time, not alone, but with God at her side; with the wisdom of His word always foremost in her mind.

In a matter of weeks she would be heading home with her husband to spend Christmas with her family back on the farm in Ontario where she had grown-up. In fact, there were relatives in the general area who had lived close by since she herself was a child - and even before. And her sister and brother-in-law lived just down the road, or across the field from the home that was so familiar to them all; the family farm.

In reality it would be a great opportunity to extend that special forgiveness she needed to exercise with Carl. But there would be much to plan before that event, and so many things to consider, including how she would approach the man while trying to appear 'normal' and friendly. In reality, nothing needed to be said. But even though she knew it was a must, the very act of forgiving from her heart seemed impossible as the time grew closer. Of course, the details of her thoughts and even her anticipation was kept to herself for obvious reasons. But the worry wouldn't leave her or let-up for even a minute.

While thoughts and the act of forgiveness had held her hostage for almost 25 years, she made the trip north with Dave to spend the Christmas holiday with close family. Over time there were things she had already come to terms with; perspectives and how those early events had affected her life choices in various situations. But the drive home was quiet, her husband never aware of all that was going-on in her mind. Over the miles she looked out the window as fields white with winter snow passed before her eyes. She was in reality oblivious to everything else around her, being consumed with thoughts of how she would approach the man again in this family setting. It was still a time of secrets left in the pockets of who she was as a person, and by their very nature couldn't be shared with anyone. And that fact alone gave added pressure to a set of circumstances she had been running from. It had been an experience she wanted to escape from, but by the closeness of ties and the influence it held over her, she would be forever held by it until she could release him. And herself. She knew she must make that move. It was critical on so many levels, and necessary for her to put that awful ordeal in its place; accepted, understood and forgiven. She had to move-on with her life.

The hours in the car gave her time to think and address the apprehension she was facing. Still, she had no choice but to struggle-on alone with it all.

The day after they arrived they would make a visit to her sister's house close by, where Barb was naturally looking forward to seeing Carol and Dave again. They were close, and, along with mom, stayed in-touch throughout the year. She was of course looking forward to the celebration they would all share-in over the season, and it would be wonderful after not seeing them since their visit back in the summer. But now they were there; there in the house and with Carl looking-on. Deep within though Carol was filled with anxiety with the thought of greeting him again. Inside she dealt with the feelings that simply would not go away; the anger and regret; the times that left her confused and empty. Hurting. But in her heart and in the silence she prayed for the strength to greet him with forgiveness and acceptance - and with a warm embrace.

He was standing behind her sister as Carol and Dave walked through the door that morning. Barb greeted them first, arms extended with a warm, welcoming embrace and loving acceptance. There was such affection and joy in her voice as she spoke, saying she was so glad they were home again. After the initial hello's and warm inviting response, Carol took a deep breath as she looked over and into the eyes of Carl himself. He was standing just behind his wife, eager to get into the picture. It was a stressful moment, but she found herself almost automatically saying "Hi Carl." "Hi Kiddo," he said, staring back at her.

She made her way over to where he was standing, reaching-out to hug him. He responded, kissing her on the cheek while giving a little squeeze. She pulled back and allowed Dave to step-in and shake his hand, thankful for the chance to break away from the closeness. No doubt she felt a disappointment in herself for the coolness that still gripped her; for the anxiety that choked her viscera like a giant fist. But it was honest. She had worked hard to close the door on her past, and especially on the event that still clung to her like threads of a spider's web. She remembered being wrapped in the silk of his seduction, where there was no escape, and at her early age, no way of dealing with or understanding what had really transpired those years ago.

The visit continued with talk throughout the afternoon, and with Carl, as always trying his best to navigate and control the conversation with his particularly arrogant attitude and tone of voice. It could be, and truly was tiring and frustrating. But the ice had been broken, although inside she felt her heart was tearing apart, for seeing him again; listening to him speak and smelling that same familiar cologne brought back memories that ate away at her. It was unbelievably difficult. She could only hope and pray God would help her come to terms with what had been done. She needed more strength than she felt capable of, although she struggled to put-on a good face, and to show a smile and some level of acceptance. The stress and pressures through the afternoon must have been intense beyond belief. It was obvious she still needed Time.

The forgiveness she had so well intended to exercise just didn't happen that Christmas. They would return home with nothing resolved in that sense, yet for Carol there was an increasing sensitivity to the opportunity that had been missed. Part of the problem was she had felt or believed that to forgive was somehow akin to accepting his behavior and actions as "O.K." But of course that's not at all what was expected. Nothing could condone what had unfolded those years ago. Then much later, and after numerous sermons on the topic, she came to realize that 'forgiveness' was not an act of condoning a wrong-doing; rather it was a condition of the heart that allowed the hurt to be freed. It allowed the individual to take-off the yoke of 'victim' and take-back control of her Life.

Over time she was able to make that move; to release him from what had caused so much distress and grief to her. She found herself with God's help finally able to say it. To do it. She didn't have to trust him necessarily. Nor did she have to forget. But she needed to forgive. And she finally did. With it she freed herself and released the bitterness that had built-up inside her. In so-doing she found herself blessed with a peace she could never have imagined, and felt a love she had never known before. The love of Jesus was overwhelming, and this experience itself helped her understand and feel what love truly meant; realizing for the first time the tremendous power it has over hate and distrust. And with this feeling filling her very heart, she was at last able to cast-off the burden that had plagued, ruled and controlled her for so long. It was as if a debt had been paid. And with thoughts of His Redemption, Salvation and Deliverance, there would be no doubt in her mind that it had. She was finally free.

Chapter Sixteen

LIBERTY

ALTHOUGH THERE WOULD BE DIFFICULTIES AND CHALLENGES in her life, Carol was blessed with a renewed sense of peace. Through her devotion to a new-found faith, she continued to seek God's help in every part of her life. And she knew her need to work on the problem with alcohol and its abuse. Carol was well aware it was hurting every aspect of her existence and somehow it had to be resolved. Its use and the behavior it encouraged had to come to a stop. She struggled mightily with it, and at every opportunity took it to the alter to lay the addiction at His feet. She would pray; even weep through what sometimes seemed like hours that overwhelmed her, waiting patiently for an answer. She wanted; needed to be delivered from the scourge of how it had effected her life and the life of her family. It was insidious in the extreme. Merciless and all-consuming.

Finally, one day at the alter, and after prayer, she began to feel a new sense of power and a special courage to both face and overcome her dependence on taking a drink. Clearly, she remembered something shifting in her thinking, and after that experience, she no longer felt the desire to indulge. The open bottle she still had remained in her closet for weeks, which would certainly not have happened before this event. In fact, she never took another drink from it. At last she felt the freedom from the hold liquor had on her life, and, after searching, went about removing other bottles that had been hidden - pouring the contents down the sink. The desire was completely and totally withdrawn, and through His promise, she had finally been delivered from its grasp.

One evening in church she gave her testimony, exposing the whole story of her battle with the bottle and the toll it had taken on her life. It was an incredibly emotional moment, giving others the opportunity to offer their own testimonies of deliverance from sickness, pain and despair. The hurts were being healed and being replaced by a peace only He could give. The change of course impacted heavily on her marriage, restoring it and breathing new life into what had, over the recent years become almost lifeless and cold partly because of the doubts and mistrust that still plagued her; where every motive was in question. It served to give her an abiding feeling of deep insecurity and even fear. A fear of what the future held and what surprises there was in store. While month after month God showed her what she needed to do to re-build a brokenness she had been living with. The suffering at last was coming to an end and she was finding a greater patience with issues in her personal life and relationships. The communication was positive, gentle and constructive, conducive to a greater tolerance and level of understanding. Where previously she could ignite into screaming, now she was quiet or even silent, recognizing the importance of this new way of living.

New pathways had been opened, and she was more determined than ever those doors would never close again.

The time since the bible study had seen Carol's life change dramatically. She was no longer the confused woman looking for answers, but rather one filled with a knowledge and an awareness that had not only changed her, but that was also influencing the lives of those around her. She realized she was not anymore an island unto herself, but rather a light that others would see - and be led to, for the gospel message had in truth come to rest in her heart. She was in fact truly saved; her life transformed by His word. She finally felt the total love and presence of God in her life, and knew the power it would have in every area of her existence. The hope she had longed for had become a reality. And it gave her the strength to move-on.

At last, the power of her addiction to alcohol had finally been removed from her life, and she had confidence God could deliver her from the last two strongholds that really prevented her from growing in her faith. She still faced the strongholds of television and the almost seductive aspects of her career. They both held her in their grasp, threatening her time with the qualities, joys and rewards they seemed to offer. Television was intensely entertaining, especially after a hard day or week at work. In some way it represented another addiction, for in reality she found herself glued to a screen that offered the good, the bad and the ugly. Instead of selecting programs of particular interest, the programming she followed became hallucinatory and almost hypnotic, regardless of their content. It consumed much of her free time, and precious moments away from her husband

and his needs. While it filled a void in the evening or through a dark night of the soul, providing perhaps a small transitory comfort over the hours, it came with a terrible cost to lives waiting to be put together; to be reassembled in the light of what she had come to know through God. It had become a serious addiction in itself, and Carol was very aware of that. But it was hard to shake. She had of course contemplated getting it out of the house. But there were other things to consider, such as her husband Dave's needs and enjoyment.

Somehow she knew God would help her with this issue too. Of course there were difficulties and endless questions, but while alcohol was not welcomed now in the house, television was. It was a problem looking for an answer. Of the two other challenges she had been facing, she felt she could realistically only handle one at a time. And 'television' would be the first to be addressed.

Carol and Dave had a cottage on a lake in southern Ontario and they would sometimes spend quality time there over the summer months, and when not in use by the family they would make arrangements to rent it out. But as cottages tend to be, it demanded a great deal of attention. Things have to be maintained inside and out, and that year she would spend her week's summer vacation getting it ready for tenants. While there one day, she decided to turn-on the television after working to get the cottage in shape. To her surprise, it didn't turn-on. She was startled and puzzled. Being used to the entertainment it provided wherever she may be, she found it distressing. Probably even empty in some way. But that was the reality of the moment. It was in a word, broken. It either had to be repaired - or replaced. Ideally as quickly as possible. As it happened, the television set was old and not really worth the cost of repair, and so the only option left would be the buying of a new one.

With their home in Western Ontario being in the country, the summer was mostly a busy time of looking after the house close to the city and the property; yard work and general up-keep. It was very demanding, and they took every opportunity to maintain it during those months. Since they were so busy around their regular home, Dave suggested they take the tele-vision they had down to the cottage by the lake. It was thought it wouldn't be missed with all the work they needed to finish. Within a couple of months they thought they could quite easily bring it back, ready for a winter of use through the hours after work and on the weekends. Then for certain it would be a very necessary part of their lives again; especially for Carol. So it was decided by both to take their own set down to the cottage for the season and for the tenants use. It would of course be missed, but it was only for ten weeks, and then it would be back home where it belonged. Carol was naturally apprehensive about losing it even for that short time. And most of us can well-understand those feelings for we get so used to its convenience. It's just a part of the household for many of us, and if we're honest, not a few of us would seriously miss it if it were gone.

Although they would have it back in the Fall, for Carol it would continue to be a challenge without it. She was deep-ly stressed and no doubt frustrated when she gave it more thought. But she knew well how easily it could take her away from God. She knew the things she had surrendered her time to - world events and attitudes disguised as entertainment - were in themselves diametrically opposed to the behaviors and beliefs she now embraced. And the struggles she found herself in she believed were not 'coincidental'. She knew God was reaching-out to guide her through the challenges she had been dealing with in her walk toward a totally different life than she had ever known before. Still, that other side of her; that very human side we all try desperately to control, not only wanted it back in her home, but seemed to need what it had to offer and the comfort and perhaps relief it provided over the long hours. But again she was well-aware it had, like other things such as her job robbed her of her time - time away from reading The Word, prayer and study, and events related to church.

It had contributed in no small way to taking her focus off other things too, including her marriage, and moments needed to give Dave more of her attention; of herself. She knew and sensed he needed greater support from his wife and partner. Viewing television though over the years had moved-on from watching shows of particular interest; wholesome programs on Nature, Discovery and her passion for diving - to watching anything available, no matter the subject or quality of the broadcast. One hour would move into another and another, and she had succumbed completely to the power it held over her. She had lost the ability to discriminate, and found herself almost hypnotized with whatever happened to be showing. She had become totally addicted to it, and the effect it was having on her life was devastating. It had to go, whatever the cost. And it did.

She had the most refreshing experience over the next while. Perhaps in a way she never could have expected. With the T.V. finally out of the house, she began to fill her evenings with things that included talking with Dave and simply helping him with a multitude of chores. Home was becoming a more peaceful place with meals being made and housework being addressed and taken care-of. A totally new commitment was evident. She started getting home from work earlier than usual, stopping for nothing or noone but the desire to share a new togetherness with her husband. Timely meals became commonplace and she noticed a more relaxed atmosphere about the house. It must have been wonderful to feel the change; the difference a new lifestyle was making to them as a couple.

It didn't take long for her to realize how God had moved to take away the distractions that prevented her from doing what God wanted to accomplish in her life. It would be one step at a time, but progress was obvious and exciting. And so that summer moved-on with the usual routines and demands of their place outside the city; the endless tasks that needed their time and effort. She quickly became thankful for the hours that had not been taken or wasted in front of the television. Her level of guilt was reduced considerably, and the nights knew a peace that simply wasn't there before. At last, she saw things being completed around her, and felt the satisfaction of what was being accomplished. She found time to read her Bible; time to pray, surrounded in a new-found tranquility. The marriage gained new strength and trust; a more focused commitment as Dave saw the calmness and joy in his wife. A wind had blown into and through a relationship, bringing a fresh environment of peace and a satisfaction that breathed love once more into their marriage. Before they knew it, the end of another season began showing its colors and Fall was upon them once again. The tenants would be leaving the cottage, and they took advantage of it by going-up on weekends to enjoy the dying embers of a long hot summer. Finally their weekends could be enjoyed together, and being there with each-other had a different feeling than ever before. They found time to talk and share, recalling those years past when they spent so much time in that beautiful place.

On the very last weekend of their stay they started to close everything down in readiness for the coming winter. So many things needed to be done, with some things collected that needed to be taken home. Dave, looking about, suddenly picked-up the television and loaded it onto the truck as originally planned. He commented that it should be taken back to the house because he didn't know how the cold temperatures would affect it at the cottage. There would be no heat all winter, and they wouldn't be back to check things out until perhaps the following Spring. Carol felt she couldn't really argue the situation, although she must surely have felt the pressures inside of possibly having the set sitting in their living-room once again - ready to exert its power. Regardless, in truth she believed she was feeling strong enough to resist putting it to use. She had reached the point where she was almost certain she couldn't be tempted, even if it was sitting in front of her. The time away from it; those weeks where they'd been so very busy had proved she could survive without it. Even flourish while feeling the freedom from its influence. In fact, she had enjoyed the extra time she found herself with, and had taken pains to use it wisely.

Sadly, as things will sometimes happen, the T.V. found its way back into the house, and she was once again unwittingly drawn to all it had to offer. No matter how much she tried - and she did, she found herself again glued to the set night after night, resulting in less time spent with her Bible and related studies - less time for things she needed to do, including household demands and prayer. Consequently she found it necessary to try to catch-up with it all at church, including her time in devotion which at home anyway had almost come to a stop because of her focus on whatever would catch her attention on the tube. Unfortunately again that was almost anything; any subject, topic or presentation. She was again captured; addicted to all it had to offer, no-matter the content. The violence, fear, horror and brutality became normal viewing, along with the lifestyles depicted and the language that colored every questionable program. Of course she would struggle with it daily, realizing what again was happening to her and the recent commitment she had made to take back the time. It had become the idol of her life once more, and she couldn't live without it. She turned to God and asked for help, knowing alone she couldn't win this battle. She needed Him to bring her to a place where she could find satisfaction in seeing it out of her life once more, this time for good.

But there was also Dave to consider. He too would often spend time in front of it, although not with the same passion that gripped his wife in such obsession. What reason could she give him to justify the decision to have it moved out of the house? She took the step of explaining to Dave, with thoughts about their earlier conversation of buying a new one eventually. In truth she really didn't want to invest in a new one. In fact, searching for his feelings on it, she finally suggested they simply take this one out of the house - and consider buying a new one just for the cottage sometime in the Spring. Seeing as they were in the process of renovating the house, she shared her belief they needed to spend more time on fixing-up all the areas needing attention, repair or even replacement. Now would not be a good time anyway to introduce a new set into the home. They would be just too busy, and it would be distracting to say the least.

There was a sigh of relief when her husband fully agreed. She could at last rid herself of the guilt of taking away his entertainment after a hard days work. He thought too it was a wonderful idea. And so together they labored to complete work on the house, finding time even to focus on the needful habits that contributed to her spiritual growth. A sense of peace once again settled about the home, and she strongly felt the blessing of His touch and guidance. God had moved. And she had obeyed. And a promise was kept.

The one remaining issue left to challenge her now was that of her career. And she would face it head-on, but only some time later when she would be confronted with something beyond what she might ever have imagined. And surely, this would result in a test to her faith beyond what she could ever have suspected. It was in many ways the ultimate challenge, and the outcome could well have cost her, her very life. And in fact it very nearly did.

Chapter Seventeen

TRUTH, TRIALS AND TRIBULATION

DAVE'S FATHER HAD TAKEN A TURN FOR the worse. Tragically, he was suffering from pancreatic cancer, and in the province of Ontario it seemed there was little more they could do for him. With hopes of being able to try new ways of dealing with it, including medications not allowed into Canada, he'd made the decision to move to Florida to take advantage of whatever their health-care system might offer. He was naturally hopeful a new approach might make the difference. The climate also would be kinder, and overall, the environment on every level would be more positive and encouraging.

Carol, along with her husband Dave flew down to visit him, hoping to provide a sense of family as well as some much-needed encouragement. And so it did. He naturally appreciated their being with him and showing the affection and love that could also help make the difference. It would not only give him added emotional and psychological strength, but also a sense of hope for the trial he was going through. That kind of support was crucial to his treatment and it couldn't help but make a difference to his feelings and the sense of caring they had brought with them. They would do everything in their power to help.

The days were hot and humid in most of that State, but like so many others they would struggle through and find time during the week's stay to keep as cool and dry as they possibly could. For Carol, who was used to working in hot summer weather when she was living at the farm, suddenly found herself becoming excessively weak and tired. She was feeling run-down and exhausted, resorting to spending more time in her hotel room under the cooling breeze of a large ceiling fan. At first she thought it was just the reality of the oppressively hot humid sub-tropical weather that would eventually move-on. She tried to convince herself it was just temporary. After all, she prided herself on not really being affected by the heat and humidity of a summer - no matter where it may be. It hadn't ever bothered her in the past. She also knew she was strong and healthy; a young woman who was ready for anything nature could throw at her. She would over the days think on it and believe for the most part it was circumstantial. Perhaps it was the left-overs of a busy time on the job and the pressures she had been under.

After some time with Dave's father, and with a promise to return, they headed back to Canada and to the usual challenges of home and office and a host of commitments that couples have to face on a daily basis. But it was time to get back to work for both of them and to catch-up with the chores they had left behind. As they did, nothing had changed for Dave who continued to suffer pain himself on a daily basis. Often it was totally debilitating, but he struggled and worked through it as much as he could. Sadly, nothing seemed to work for the agony he had dealt with so long, and he got by for a while on pain-killers and muscle relaxants. He was eventually diagnosed with Fibromyalgia. Still, relief of any sort was only temporary at best. But as it happened even that focus was about to be altered in ways that couldn't be remotely expected. And both their lives were to change because of it.

Carol's fatigue and exhaustion after returning from Florida was in the end symptomatic of something unimaginable at the time. Settling-in from their trip, she began to experience a numbness in her left foot. Soon it was progressing slowly up into her leg until it reached her knee. Then the other foot started to follow, and shortly they realized there was no choice but to seek attention at the nearest Emergency Department. After Dave's earlier experience, and the months finding help for his own condition, he took control of the situation by driving her there, seeing her difficulty and worry trying to deal with this frightening development. It was obviously serious and in no way normal. Once there, and after thoroughly examining her, the physicians couldn't come to any conclusion about her condition. As a result, the visit simply resulted in their being told to return if the situation worsened. They left the hospital still concerned as to just what the problem could be, while naturally assuming had it been serious, surely they would have known.

Within a couple of weeks the numbness had started to climb in both legs until it reached her waste, and so again they set-off for the hospital. During this second examination and questioning, she explained it had now progressed in both legs. Emotionally, it would have been a fearful time for them both with this development. This time though, the doctors set to work with more in depth tests, and with a determination to get to the bottom of it all. There had to be a cause. Unfortunately, once again they were told they had no answers for the problem. It simply could not be explained, and they were sent packing, into the unknown and with understandable apprehension. It seemed even the trained medical community could not help. It had become very serious, and when you are facing it alone - without help, it can fill one's heart with fear.

There would be the endless nights of suffering and worry; worry as to what was happening in her body; concern over the apparent reality that nothing could be done. The condition; whatever she was stricken with wasn't even understood. We can only imagine the distress they must have experienced through this awful trial. And there was no-where they could turn for understanding or relief from the grip of this unknown disease, if that's in fact what it was. In truth, they were lost in a quagmire of circumstance, trying to make sense or come to terms with whatever the affliction was. The stress during this time was immense, challenging every part of her life and that of her husband; lives that were changing to accommodate the sickness she was struggling with. In the unsafe and frightening darkness of our thoughts, when we are most vulnerable, fear has a way of creeping into every part of our being. It is a lonely feeling that can begin as a cry deep inside; a smothered sound that grows louder and yet cannot be heard by another. It can choke one into despair, leaving one helpless and abandoned and emotionally destitute; the earlier options laying still and cold along the floor. It is surely the very pit of hopelessness.

They returned to the hospital a third time when the numbness continued to progress up to her chest. This time though, Dave refused to leave until something was confirmed. During this particular examination, and after looking over her chart, he shared with them the fact that previously no attempts had been made to treat the symptoms she had gone-in with before. Apparently, comments made on her chart made the suggestion that the symptoms were, to quote, "all in her head." It was both devastating and disappointing to hear that, after she had been suffering so acutely from some obvious physical difficulty. Now, having been off work for a few weeks already, her husband was livid with the casual and unprofessional approach the physicians had taken. They demanded more, insisting on answers and action before the situation worsened even more. This time the attending doctor called for a CAT scan and blood work as well as a spinal tap. With them finally giving her condition serious attention, they admitted her to hospital in order to monitor her closely.

The following morning the doctors came into her room to let her know the outcome of all the tests. The results were not good, and what was said would drive their very existence for the next five years at the exclusion of everything else. This would be the start of the endless trips to appointments and bouts of disability, resulting in Carol being off work for months at a time. She was diagnosed with Transverse Myelitis; an infection of the spinal column. It was August of 2008. At this point in time there was no way of knowing the source of the infection, but it was taking a dreadful toll on her. Consequently they started a regimen of intravenous steroids, but it was really the other information they shared with her that struck fear through her heart. Because of the symptoms she experienced, along with their inability to explain the infection and its cause, they left her with a note of caution. She would remember their words no doubt for the rest of her life.

"There is a possibility you may have Multiple Sclerosis, and what we are seeing could well be the initial signs. We'll treat the infection. The steroids will reduce the inflammation and it's possible you could totally recover from this anyway."

They continued to tell her that if the symptoms re-occurred - and should they be any different from what she had, and be in a different part of her body over the following six months - it would be likely she had Multiple Sclerosis. Even the thought of it was deafening. The words brought visions of people she'd seen with M.S. Pictures showed the victims in wheel-chairs or severely disabled. Carol was only 46 at the time and no-one in her family has suffered this disease. It left her confused and obviously worried for there seemed to be no answers or any explanation. On top of it all, she had always been strong and healthy and never showed any indication of any serious illness other than ulcers when she was young.

She was placed on intravenous steroids for the next two weeks, and while M.S. was not the diagnosis that day, it may as well have been. As a couple, they felt the threat of it looming over their heads like a weight that could tip and fall at any moment, shattering their lives for good. Their days and all of their thoughts were consumed with reading and studying everything they could on that dreaded disease, and with each line read, the fear continued to grow. She naturally imagined every scenario, from being extremely disabled and wheel-chair bound to living far below the dreams they had hoped and planned for over the previous years. Looking into the information available, there were many factors in her life that could impact and even encourage the progress of M.S. The one that had been discussed, and that stuck-out above so many others was the issue of stress. It is one of the greatest triggers to its progression, and should be avoided in every possible way. Both Carol and Dave were aware the stress from her job was horrific and must be reduced and avoided at all costs. After reaching this point in their search for a cure - though no such thing existed for Multiple Sclerosis, her husband, while covering his feeling very well, was devastated. Together they made every effort to maintain composure because after all, at this moment in Time, the disease was only a possibility. They had to find strength together; to be patient in their struggle, and to keep abreast of any new information that might help over the coming months.

For the moment, the steroids were doing their job and most of the numbness seemed to have left, although some still was evident in her feet. For the most part though it was minor compared to what it had been, and even tolerable. With this improvement she returned to work, and for a few months anyway, Life was basically and thankfully normal. But naturally, there remained that nagging relentless thought in the back of her mind, and any ache or pain; any even subtle change in her body would trigger thoughts of whether this was "it". Was this hurt or that discomfort a furthering symptom the doctors had threatened could be confirming the diagnosis of M.S.? Through the experience, and the dark hours we suffer through alone, even as a couple, they would talk and Dave would try to comfort her through each trial. But it would be so overwhelming. And it was difficult to maintain a front when a dreaded disease may be lurking ever closer to taking her. The mind can only handle so much pressure; so much apprehension and fear. Carol had not told her family of the doubts she still had in her own mind. She'd mentioned only the infection in her spine, comforting them by saying the course of steroids had been correcting it and otherwise, everything was just fine.

She continued going to work under this incredible pressure. In fact that was the thing that was paramount - the disabling realty of an extremely stressful job with enormous responsibility - and whose demands seemed to increase exponentially as each day went by. By now it really was a case of survival on a daily basis - even by the hour at times. The feelings that would consume her through this time were crippling in their own way; debilitating as they ran rampant through her mind and body, and the evenings brought little comfort with the constant reminders of her condition. She would read and ponder the articles about Multiple Sclerosis, where warnings were repeated again and again of the impact of stress on her health. No matter what else she did, it had to be reduced; minimized because of what it could trigger in her now weakened and vulnerable body. Her immune system seemed out of control and could well run right off the tracks unless something could be done. When stress becomes so severe and prolonged, it creates chronic inflammatory conditions, allowing the system to be particularly susceptible to autoimmune diseases.

In reality she was afraid of a relapse into her old state she had struggled with over the months, and she knew each relapse had the potential of further impacting her mobility.

It was a horrifying thought. At her job, tasks that at one time were straight-forward and commonplace, generated both anxiety and frustration, sometimes bringing her to tears. She would find herself sitting at her computer trying to type-out a simple email that was once done with such ease and confidence. Now there was only hesitation and uncertainty. But her studies for a business degree had prepared her well for the skills needed to do the job under normal conditions, and while always coming with a high level of stress, it had been manageable up until now. At this time though, her ability to cope with even the simplest of tasks was trying her in every way. It was both frightening and discouraging, taking away whatever hope she held onto. In truth it had all become too much. The situation had become critical, and obviously she couldn't continue for very long under such duress. She was weakening, and struggling to hold-on, knowing only God could help her out of the valley. Through the darkness of the experience, Carol would share her feelings with Dave as they reached-out to each-other in support. As a husband, he felt helpless and shattered not being able to give answers or even the guidance his wife needed. It all seemed so hopeless and cold. It had in fact become a lonely excursion into a world of shadows and a certain unreality. He was desperately worried about her and their future unless things were to change. In turn, she felt his need and deep concern, understanding the anguish that gripped them as they walked together through a crisis that seemed to have no end. And in the quiet moments of despair, she prayed and thought on that wonderful Psalm 121 - "*I will lift-up mine eyes unto the hills from whence cometh my help.*"

Whatever the outcome over the coming weeks and months, her very survival had been reduced to that simple reality of another cry to God. She needed Him and His comfort to face the coming truths; the trials and tribulations. She needed His love, and the strength of her faith perhaps more than ever before.

Chapter Eighteen

MULTIPLE SCLEROSIS

A FEW MONTHS PASSED, AND CAROL STARTED having problems with her vision. She thought at first it was probably from the strain of the demands at work and the time spent on the computer. But she also found it increasingly difficult to type, and this was a major part of her job. She was good at it, having done it for the past 28 years with great skill and accuracy, her fingers flying over the keyboard with aplomb and confidence. In other words, she was a natural. Suddenly though she found herself making errors that were out of the ordinary for her, and she grew increasingly anxious with tasks she once took-on with great ease and flair. Her sight continued to change over a short period of time to the point where she was having double vision, and her peripheral vision had become distorted as well. It was a frightening experience, allowing the mind to run rampant with thoughts 0f other things that might have gone wrong; especially issues related to her earlier diagnosis just months before. She made an appointment to see her optometrist, seeing what clearly appeared to be problems with her eyes. Once there, and amongst the questions asked was, "Have you had any changes to your health at all?"

Of course she took the time to explain all she had gone through over the months, along with the diagnosis of Transverse Myelitis and the information shared by the physicians there was the possible risk of Multiple Sclerosis looming over the health care concerns. The optometrist continued with the examination, and after a while explained that in fact he was seeing changes to her vision which didn't look good. It was at this point he insisted strongly she seek medical attention immediately. Although not spoken, Carol already suspected he was thinking of the distinct possibility of her having M.S. But only further and more in-depth testing could confirm such a condition. Looking back on what she had been told earlier in the hospital, she was in fact experiencing "different symptoms" - and in a different part of her body; and all occurring within the six month period they had warned her of. The threat was palpable and frightening, for she would naturally think and remember reading that if this were to happen; if the disease was able to take hold of her, there was no cure. There would be only a continuing deterioration into a world too dreadful to even think about. She was still a young woman with a whole lifetime ahead of her, and with a mind and heart full of dreams she had shared with her husband. The future had looked so full and rich and exciting. Almost endless in its possibilities. But now it was put on pause until these physical changes could be explained.

Carol worked very hard not to over-react to the threat she was dealing with, although it was naturally overwhelming. In reality, it had become all too personal and difficult for both of them, and they had no choice but to return to the Emergency Department they had last visited.

In conversation with the doctors, the 'history' of their prior findings was repeated, with them looking once again at the tests that had been repeated. After only a brief consultation, they did not drag their heals this time. They scheduled her for an immediate MRI.

With Dave beside her in the emergency room, they waited in silence, intensely aware of the noises; unfamiliar noises and sounds that seemed to drift around and about them, only to disappear after a while into the background. But they would be replaced by others that would prick the senses with distress and even despair while waiting for news from the medical team. Time would have passed slowly, and looking back, she couldn't recall exactly how long they waited, but she does remember being moved from one room to another as more patients were admitted.

During this time her thoughts turned to God and His presence in her life that had over that short time made such a difference. She thought on His love and all that He had done for her - not only in a very personal way, with feelings, values, beliefs and goals, but also within her marriage. Carol knew in her heart that had she faced all of this before she had come to know and trust Him, she would have long crumbled under the weight of the struggle. She knew all too well she would have been reaching for a bottle, and not the hand of God to guide her. With these thoughts upper-most in her mind, she found reassurance that whatever the outcome, God was with her. He had proven to be faithful over the preceding years, convincing her she was not alone in the struggle - and that there was in the end, a purpose to it all. She remembered pieces from the Bible; the witnesses, and how great men of faith had been tested, coming through victoriously. Together they gave her the strength she needed to face the challenges coming at her, and a certainty in knowing God would give her all that she needed to overcome - and to see His purpose fulfilled.

Suddenly the silence was broken when doctors appeared from behind the curtain where she was laying. There were two of them this time, giving Carol immediate concern with their combined presence - as if carrying her very life in their hands. And in a way they were. Surely the news couldn't be good, with more than one coming to her side. Looking up at them, she waited for a comment; a word or any explanation that could give encouragement. Within the span of a single breath one of them proceeded to explain what had been realized from the examination. He wanted to remind them of what they had suggested and warned them of after the previous tests. The tension was palpable and unbearable. But he went on to describe details of their previous diagnosis of Transverse Myelitis, repeating for them the risks they had faced with a possibility of M.S. But now they had the results of the MRI. And this was the focus of his comments. They had in fact found lesions on her brain. It was finally confirmed:

"Carol, you have Multiple Sclerosis."

Slowly turning her head, she looked into her husband's face, almost feeling her very life slipping out of control. Stunned. Overwhelmed, and coping with a feeling of utter helplessness.

It was an emotion that would fill her senses over the coming months. Now the tears welled-up in her eyes as she tried to come to terms with the diagnosis, and in truth, she didn't know what to say. Thoughts, feelings and emotions would have been intense and painful, leaving no place for words. She saw the pain in her husband's eyes, telling her once again just how much he loved her. They held hands. Tightly. Holding on to their own private thoughts while choking on the reality of what they had been told. For minutes of a silence that was already too loud, they listened to more of the details shared by the team. After the essential statement had been made, and the patient made aware of what she was dealing with, the physician explained the first course of short-term treatment she could expect, including another round of intravenous steroids for three weeks to allevi-ate the symptoms and give her a degree of comfort. After, Dave asked the questions that flooded into his mind, many coming from the material they had read over the months, but most from the desperate feelings they had shared as a couple. The worry and apprehension; the not-knowing. The sense of being alone with it all. They had talked often and researched the condition, hoping of course the outcome would be survivable.

In the curtained rooms of a hospital department, reserved for the crippled souls of a humanity suffering an illness, there were sounds that were personal and vulgar, that fell onto the floor with the ring of pan or a whispered cry. And "voices dying with a dying fall" through a trauma that screamed from a stillborn dream, ringing like a stone caught in a pipe some-where down the hall. Where and how might it all end. What had been presented and explained, promised to change the life they had known together. And for the moment, it seemed the future lay prostate and lost in a strange 'no man's land' where even our boldest musings are afraid to tread.

Carol knew well, as did her husband, the effects stress makes on such a disease. A major trigger, and to be avoided at all costs. A million things drifted in and out of her mind over the moments as she tried to come to terms with the diagnosis; the reality of what was to be the rest of her life. But the fight was in her even then, as was the awareness of God's presence both in the past and in the present. Under extreme duress, we naturally flow through every facet of the human condition, into strength and through the rumblings of a vulnerability that under terms, comes to grip us by the throat when we walk too far from His word. Along with others, the words and promise in Psalm 34:19 would have come to mind through the dark moments of the day, *"Many are the afflictions of the righteous; but the Lord delivers him out of them all."* She would cling onto every piece of scripture; every suggestion and every encouragement, for she had come to believe in the truth she had finally accepted through her readings, studies and commitment to church, and with the guidance of her trusted pastor.

But now the issue of stress was foremost on her mind after hearing the warnings of the medical team, as well as the suggestions seen in their research. It had to be addressed immediately. It can not only hasten the disease, but also result in relapses that can in the end be catastrophic. Again Carol looked over at her husband, "Dave, I really must give-up my job. The stress is just too much."

He nodded. He understood completely, and, agreeing, squeezed her hand once again to confirm his support as well as his love. They were united completely as they entered into a new walk that would test them in every imaginable way. She turned to the doctor to explain her position, describing the pressure of her work and the toll she felt it was taking on her physically.

"That's what concerns me," he said, you have to avoid it in any way you can. You have to work at reducing it, because right now that's the greatest threat to your condition. Unchecked it could have a profound effect on your health. Might be a good time to consider an alternative career where the demands would be less. On a practical level, I know it's not an easy thing to do, but you must find a way together."

"Together," she thought, as her eyes turned back to her husband. The word seemed different now under these new circumstances. It had a different sound somehow. A different taste. An added feeling. Certainly a comfort. She knew Dave would do anything to help. That was a given. It was critical she move as far away as possible from the stress she dealt with so that her energy could be directed toward healing and simply moving forward with the treatment they were planning for her. She had reached the point where she had no choice but to consider a new career where the pressures would be significantly reduced. It was essential if she were to survive this awful experience.

The short conversation with the doctor was really all she needed to hear, and it echoed in her heart as if from God himself. Change. In some way he had already made that decision for them. Now they just had to buy into it with all they had, and see what could be done. With her mind made-up, she would dialogue with Dave and her boss about the possibilities of finding something - another position hopefully within the company she already worked for.

It seemed only moments ago that the handsome compensation her job offered; the security and bonuses was paramount to their happiness and lifestyle. But no longer. Her health had become their priority. She simply wanted to be well. The high-status positi0n she held, and the power and influence it exercised no longer mattered. So much had changed after the diagnosis, and the first step already taken with their decision to downgrade the income and improve her working as well as her home environment.

Through the intense emotions that developed over a period of time as she struggled with how the rest of her life might be approached, there was something quite unique that pushed its way to the surface; something which Carol herself would have been surprised at in the beginning. With thoughts often in high gear and forever busy with the recent challenges, she realized that in fact she was never really fearful of the disease and the outcome. Although she prayed fervently for the symptoms that relentlessly battered her weakened body, she never did pray for the healing. Rather Carol became focused on what the disease might accomplish in her life and the lives of others. From scripture she remembered the trials of Joseph as he went from the pit, in which his brothers had cast him, to being in slavery and even in prison - his rising again to be second under pharaoh himself. Each of his trials had taught him something about the next step to which God would lift him. But the real emphasis of it all was not in the greatness of Joseph himself, but in how God had blessed him as we read in Genesis 12. In its understanding, Carol felt now there was indeed a purpose to her life, and she began to pray the diagnosis of Multiple Sclerosis would in the end bring a spiritual healing to her husband Dave - that the present trial that held them both in its grasp would draw him to God as her own earlier trials had. This then had become the real focus of her prayers. Not for herself, but for her husband's salvation.

For the second time in half a year Carol was off work once again. She continued to struggle with the effects of the steroids which in themselves can have dangerous side-affects. While they do reduce inflammation in the body, they also take a toll in other ways. She continued to study not only the disease she had been diagnosed with, but also the root cause of so many others. It helped give her a better understanding of how the body is attacked through the weakest link, and how the symptoms of course may well vary with each individual. For her own condition, she began to feel it may have been triggered by the early use of alcohol at the age of thirteen, along with the abuse of tobacco which she'd smoked for over fifteen years. There was also the thought that poor diet, and later, extreme stress had weakened her immune system, bringing it to the edge - and eventually overwhelming her system which had become run-down and vulnerable.

Regardless of the details, the silent pressures had made themselves known and taken-over her body in a most vicious struggle, resulting in the fight of her life. Now, after a couple of months away from work, the steroids had given some relief and brought her physically to a stronger place where she could face the daily challenge once again. She decided to return to work and do the best she could. But there was always the thought and fear that clung to her very being - not knowing if and when the next relapse would strike. It was a dreadful load to carry through such a difficult time, and she would cope the best she could, pushing with great determination through the feelings and conversations that would find their way into her thoughts as one day moved into another.

In so many ways, it would be the waiting that would bring her the greatest stress during this time. Her life was in some controlled chaos; her very survival in question; the future clearly uncertain. Other aspects of her existence were pushed into the background out of necessity, and understanding the options open to her, which were very few, she realized the need to turn to the one she believed with all her heart could help. God. He would be the source of her strength through this difficult and frightening journey. It gave her the power and the ability to move-on as best she could, and would be a source of comfort for her husband Dave, seeing his wife lifted by The Word she knew she could trust. It would make all the difference for them both, and they would face the issues together - renewed and with new hope in where they might find the help and support they needed in their search. Time would tell.

Chapter Nineteen

TO EVERY THING THERE IS
A SEASON

IT WAS ALL SO NEW. DIFFERENT. As the days and weeks unfolded she worked to become accustomed to a completely new lifestyle that would have been familiar to any patient suffering from M.S. Now there were regular visits to the clinic to monitor her health. At the early stage of her condition, it was scheduled every three months to ensure she was not only checked, but educated to the disease. The work of the medical team was also essential in helping the patients handle the treatment and to ultimately identify the type of M.S. they are dealing with. There are in fact four types or courses the disease could follow. The most common is the Relapsing-Remitting M.S. which develops with clearly defined attacks of worsening neurological function. It's also characterized by unpredictable but clearly defined relapses There is the Secondary Progressive course, so-named because it follows also a particular identifiable pattern of relapsing and remitting, and the Primary Progressive type characterized by a worsening neurological functioning - but this time from the very beginning. Lastly there is the Progressive-Relapsing version that is the least common, but recognized by its steady progression. The difficulty arises here in that the 'types' often are usually not identifiable until the disease has really taken hold over a period of time. Only then would the patient become fully aware of what they are facing, and what to expect from the treatment.

While there is no actual cure for Multiple Sclerosis, the medications given are designed only to slow the progression, and to hopefully stop the most debilitating of them all - the Progressive, which tragically places the patient in a state of total dependency with no capacity to function independently. The very thought of it is intimidating and terrifying. Fully intending to stay on top of it, Carol began attending M.S. support groups to help deal with the questions, uncertainties and feelings that would flood into her mind. She needed to know what was available at that time, and how things looked in terms of the future. What if anything was on the horizon that might give her and others hope of some control. She needed to know how others coped with the disease; those who had been living with it over a longer period of time. How did they manage the symptoms; the relapses and feelings they would leave you with. She needed answers and a certain encouragement to get-on with a life that was changing faster than the seasons.

She noticed others coming to the meetings in various stages of it. Some were completely incapable of controlled body movement, being wholly dependent of their care-giver for 100% of their daily needs. Some walked with a limp, and others with a cane for support. More would arrive and appeared to be functioning, but spoke of sleepless nights from the pain and cramps, while some described the debilitating fatigue they had to endure. Then there was Carol. Relatively new to the scene. Other than the two relapses suffered, she looked by comparison a picture of health, feeling she wasn't fitting-in with what they were all struggling with. There was a sense of guilt, for as much as she struggled and worried how this would all end, she knew any person in that room would have gladly traded places with her. And such as it was, it was this experience and related incidents that caused her to think again on how far she had come in her walk with God. How she had been delivered from so much that threatened to destroy her. She realized with a new awareness she was no more insignificant to God as a child is to their father, knowing how they would gladly give-up their very life for them, and indeed, Jesus did. It filled her thoughts with the understanding of just what He did for us. This powerful perspective and belief brought more than a little comfort to the situation, no-doubt raising the confidence of them as a couple as they worked through the ordeal to find answers and the right path. Left without the presence of God in her life, the predicament would collapse into a state of confusion and despair, and the continuing struggle would have been unbearable. Now though her thoughts and prayers would sustain her and Dave through a time of frightening uncertainty, giving them the strength to go-on to find a way through this deeply personal challenge.

So much becomes clear when we live-out our lives in total faith. Carol had come to believe in every promise He had given, feeling there are no coincidences in a life committed to

God. She knew He held Eternity in His hands, along with our lives - each and every one of us - believers or not.

For Carol, and with a threatening condition taking its toll both physically as well as emotionally, she found herself undergoing significant changes in every area of her existence. No longer was she arriving home loaded down with a briefcase full of work that would consume her attention. Rather she was pulling into her driveway by the time supper should be on; a change from the late hours she had struggled through for so long. Her weekends too were freed-up to take advantage of the many things she needed to do around the house and with her husband. There were needs they both had; needs to rescue the hours from the cruel master that directs and sometimes motivates the mind and body, far away from the comfort and warmth of true affection; of a special peace and comfort - and of home. There was once more, in the brooding hours of the evening and the warming rays of the sun, a fresh awareness; an intimacy whose unshackled passion needed to reconnect in the shade of this new understanding.

In a hurried life, so much is missed and undigested in the search for success and recognition; the high financial reward we hunt through the winding streets of commerce. Now, the simple things that went unnoticed when she was wrapped so completely in the challenges of managing a large call center were suddenly making themselves known and demanding attention. But it came and appeared as a welcome requisition. Compared to what she had experienced over so many years, this approach to her past, present and future gave the opportunity to start a new course toward a destination she had only dreamed of before. She could see clearly the hand of God directing her movement through a difficult time. And all she had to do was listen and follow.

For the first time in a while and through eyes not quite so distracted, she once again began noticing Dave's needs, although he never would express them or vocalize them in any way. But of course they were there. She did whatever she could to meet them with the energy she had once used for the demands of others and especially her staff. The question would rise-up in her heart over the days, wondering if in fact he had noticed the extra effort and attention. While nothing was said, she saw and felt the evidence of it in the transformation of their relationship. The direction of their lives now had changed, along with the priorities. Such a serious diagnosis has a way of doing that. It surely was a wake-up call that was never expected; a reason to re-address the way things had been going and to take stock; smell the roses and look again at what really in the end is important. And that's what was happening during the time following the symptoms and the final diagnosis that naturally impacted them both heavily. It was in every possible way a time of transition. All it needed now was direction. And with God at the helm, she felt confident when the moment was right He would steer a course for her - and for them both, into a safe harbor.

There's no doubt it was unusual. Unexpected perhaps by the majority of us, given the dire situation she found herself in. While most of us would be in a place of uncertainty and fear, Carol, even in the early stages of the condition was already feeling an encouraging hope, although completely unaware of what the future held. While the mystery of her time going forward was unknown, she had the faith that 'someone' really did know. She knew she wouldn't be left alone with it, or forsaken. She believed with all her heart that in the end, there was a purpose that over time would bring everything into focus. There would be an understanding to the trials she was in - that they were in as a couple. In the end it would all have a meaning.

The next step for Carol was making the important decision as to the treatment she required to battle the M.S. In fact, none of the drugs used had given any hope for a cure. At best they offered some security and a degree of confidence that any relapses she might be faced with would be less severe and even less frequent. In theory, treatment of the right kind might even lessen the risk of reaching the point where doctors might indicate a movement toward the Progressive form of the disease. And for that there is no hope, only a rapid progression into a total dependence on others for the rest of your life.

After researching the suggested medications and looking into their side effects which were in themselves terrifying, together they chose Copaxone. It was taken by daily injection, and held a promise of slowing down further advancement of the condition. It also had fewer destructive side-effects than any of the others. With it there was less chance of compromising other organs of the body, and this gave her added confidence. But coming to terms with the frequent injections took some getting used-to. Giving them to herself in the forearm, stomach, buttocks and thighs, it was essential she rotate the injection sites to avoid damage to the muscle tissue. But no matter where it was given, they were painful; uncomfortable for a quarter of an hour after. She soon got into the regimen of applying ice to address the swelling and even the pain. The whole thing was a task noone would look forward to, and it would only remind her of her condition, leaving traces of not only discomfort but also an anxiety and concern for what was ahead.

As the treatment for M.S. was getting started, so was her search for that new position. It was an awful thought, imagining the need to train for a new occupation after all the years she had worked at her job. She had successfully climbed the corporate ladder without any need for interviews as she advanced in the company. Her skills, abilities and determination were sufficient in the past to gain each promotion, and the idea of competing for another position through interviews was daunting after twenty-five years in her career. So much had changed in the work place, and she had reached a point where she didn't feel confident her experience and work ethic would speak for themselves. She felt certain her search would raise questions about her motives - perhaps bringing into the picture the fact she was suffering from a dreaded disease. Was she even marketable at this time of her life, given the difficulties and problems she would be facing on a daily basis. It didn't look good, all things considered. There was so much against her from the very beginning.

Regardless she had to try. She had to find a way to reduce the high levels of stress that now promised to destroy her if her condition worsened. But would she have the strength to go-on? Again she turned to God in prayer to seek His help, His comfort and guidance. But through it all the medication she was on wasn't having a lasting impact, and that was a great concern. Fortunately she had realized some relief for a few months, but then new symptoms developed unexpectedly. There were relapses occurring on a regular basis after a while, following the treatments with the steroids. Then there was the extreme pain in her lower limbs, and cramping at night. And the fatigue; the very same concern she had heard others talk about before caused her to be off work for three months because she could barely function.

Finding the strength to even get out of bed was almost too much, and in the mornings she would have no choice but to return, climbing back after a short half hour of being up and about. Soon she was spending weeks either in bed or in the Lazy Boy doing basically nothing. In reality, there was nothing she really could do. Life now had become an exercise in survival and she wasn't at all convinced she was winning. But she found after a while she did have both the energy and the ability to do one thing; she was able to hold a book in her hands. It was an exciting possibility under those difficult circumstances. At least on this one seemingly insignificant thing, she began to experience a small degree of control. And the value and meaning of it at a time like that was a treasure she could embrace and enjoy. A blessing in every sense of the word. Given all that had unfolded into her life, and with the continued awareness of how God was working through her, she chose The

Bible to read. She thought of that special blessing and how it had made itself known as a result of that one relapse. And with all the strength she could muster, she read. And she read; completing the entire Bible from Genesis to Revelation over those hours, days and weeks. In fact, it was something she had always wanted to do, but in the past and with her demanding schedule, never had the time. It would have been impossible to describe just what it did for her faith. It grew, along with a greater understanding of God, giving her added strength and encouragement - and a developing sense of Purpose that spelled Hope through the new conditions she was facing. The experience with The Word made the difference once again in how she was seeing the trials she was under. It lifted her spirits onto a new level; a new place where she could finally engage the trust she had come to know was there for her.

She was still under the pressures and the demands of dealing with the treatment she needed. But next came the inability to sleep. She was overtaken by insomnia, and sleep completely eluded her. She would suffer the exhaustion daily, and at times could hardly function. Her faith and belief in God and His presence in her life sustained her again through those dark days that colored her life, and the life of her husband Dave. And after a time of very little sleep she had no choice but to seek medical help. This resulted as one might expect, in a physician prescribing sleeping pills. But as each prescription was filled and used, the dosage had to be increased to maintain the effect the medication had in the beginning. It was a vicious cycle of trying to stay on top of things as best she could. But the increasing demands that met her each morning; the choices and decisions she was left to make were taking a toll on her emotionally as well as physically.

Chapter Twenty

THE JOB

THERE WAS STILL THE ISSUE OF A new job to face. Although finding another position was obviously necessary, she knew it wouldn't be easy. And it's hard to give-up all you have worked for over the years; the income and prestige and the lifestyle it allowed. There's a special feeling that comes with 'having made it' after all the struggles, study and effort. But she knew the move would be critical to her health over the coming months. She knew also there was no other choice but to approach her boss about the situation she was facing - and her changing needs. And that meant having to disclose the details of her growing disability. A million thoughts would have gone through her mind as she prepared herself to meet with him. And where do you start? What should be best left-out - or included? And would she be understood? She had to take that chance, and in a leap of faith give it all she had as she prepared to present her case in finding another less stressful position. She was acutely aware whatever she ended-up doing would result in a very significant reduction in pay as well. As Carol shared and talked with her husband, the one thing they would be certain of was the significant change that was making itself known in their lives. And such uncertainty is itself full of its own protracted misgivings. The world they faced now, together, was one they could never have imagined just a short while before. And the Unknown has its own way of getting our attention as they were beginning the fight of their lives. As it happened, there was in fact only one thing she could be sure of through these harrowing times; the very nearness of God and His presence. When Carol returned to work she was understandably apprehensive at the thought of meeting with a senior administrator. She felt psychologically naked and defenseless having to discuss and reluctantly share her diagnosis with him. Really, she was totally at his mercy, and placing herself in that situation was very intimidating. She herself had worked in a significant capacity for the company, but was soon to find herself on the lowest rung of a new ladder, looking-up - hoping someone was there with a thoughtful heart; someone in a position to help, given what she was going through with her health crisis. She knew no-one would or could ever understand what she was facing with the demands that had dropped into her lap unexpectedly. She was on shaky ground, and while working heroically to push ahead with all she had to do, so much was expected of her at work and in her personal life. Often an individual can put on a face and appear confident and unconcerned. But deep inside the viscera it can be a totally different story; a battle to survive not only the physical trauma that plagues every waking moment, but also the dreadful diagnosis that threatens to define us as much as we may fight it.

Under some circumstances an individual can feel not only at odds with the new reality - but also lost; waiting to be redeemed by someone carrying within them a particular compassion. Who am I now and what have I become? You can almost hear the questions raised in the quiet hours at the end of the day when the barriers we build begin to collapse, falling from the sheer fatigue; the weight of circumstance. Sometimes when the body reels from exhaustion and the hurt, confidence and even hope bows-out and we are left with the cold undressed image of ourselves held hostage to something completely out of our control. Sometimes when we are the most vulnerable, conditions take advantage and we rally all the resources available to fight back. For Carol, already backed into a corner, she would repeatedly turn her attention to God, and the peace He promised. She would find the comfort again in His word, being moved to think on John 14:27 - "*Peace I leave with you, my peace I give unto you - not as the world giveth, give I unto you. Let not your heart be troubled, neither let it be afraid.*"

The focus itself tells so much about this young woman caught-up in a series of unimaginable events. It speaks volumes about her faith and the impact of God in her life. But it also describes her character and inner strength; a particular strength gained from the lessons of an early experience and eventual awareness, and her desire to know Jesus personally. She was now more than ever deeply aware of the need to walk the path she had come to know, for on it there was safety and salvation; and a peace that in the end would surpass all understanding. And it was this she wanted more than ever, not just for herself - but for her husband Dave as well. She would put everything she had to into the struggle. And even at this relatively early stage, she felt confident there was a purpose to her suffering. In time she knew it would be revealed. And that was enough to sustain her through that critical time while she worked to fight the disease, and as she searched for a new position. There had to be a meaning to it all.

Above all, she wanted to be fair. The change she would cause with her request for a different job would in the end put a strain on her department of over eighty people. It was a very serious responsibility. But approaching the boss now would give him time also to begin the search for a new manager. With this in mind, she did meet with him, explaining the diagnosis she had been given and the necessary steps it was suggested she take to help cope with the task of keeping it under control and stopping any further progression. She explained she was hoping to move into another position if at all possible, preferably within the company, but she would certainly consider any other offer. She also indicated she would give whatever notice he needed, but reinforced the fact that she would have no choice but to leave her present assignment.

She had only worked for this man for about a year and was surprised with the interest he showed in finding a job she could engage with; one that would fill her needs and help her through this personal crisis. He was incredibly thoughtful and understanding, and it was a tremendous relief for Carol. Of course he asked for details about her interests; the type of position she would feel comfortable with. Truth was, she wasn't that particular as long as it was below her present supervisory level. Work, status and the rewards that came with it were not a driving passion for her anymore. In fact, she couldn't wait to get as far away from that scene as quickly as she could. And whatever the job offered, she would simply have to learn to adapt, whatever the position might be. Finally, he asked Carol to send him her resume, suggesting she allow him a couple of weeks before looking elsewhere in the company.

Robert met with Carol a couple of weeks later, asking if she would be interested in a National Client Service Co-ordinator position. It didn't take her long to accept it, knowing as she did there would be a huge drop in salary, almost by a half. The very thought of it was daunting, and the reality was, their financial picture would be dramatically changed for the foreseeable future. Having done her math on what the losses might be to their combined resources, she thought-on the usual annual raises that would be given over the years. In any event, it would take considerable time to climb the economic ladder again, and there was no doubt it was a cause for worry for them both. On top of that, while Dave held a good position as well, they still carried a hefty mortgage. And there were other things to consider; the very details of living on a reduced income after twenty years of financial security. They had a lot to think about. As they talked and made attempts to understand exactly what the implications could be, and with questions as to how they could hope to manage under these new circumstances, thoughts would be driven to consider future possibilities with respect to their home. There would be things they simply would not be able to afford, but essential needs such as basic upkeep would have to be taken-care of. While this included necessary maintenance, it didn't take into account the need for further renovations as time went by. They tried to consider all events and possibilities that might arise, no matter how premature it all may have seemed. She had to consider the pressing possibility of her own future mobility with the disease. Would she be wheel-chair bound? A helpless invalid surviving life as a recluse, away from the society she knew and enjoyed? There would be changes to their home that would be required if she became disabled. And sadly, these are just a few of the pressures and fears brought-on with a diagnosis of Multiple Sclerosis.

For this moment in time, the reality was, the job opportunity was too good to pass. And she was glad to accept the offer. While the rewards were not nearly as attractive as her role in management had been, she was relieved at not having to go through a learning curve in an entirely new and unfamiliar department. It sounded ideal, and for the first time in a long time she felt some relief from the emotional and psychological stress that gripped both her and her husband. Carol was familiar with most of the work demanded in the new position, and so moving into it wouldn't present any kind of a problem for her. She would feel the relief at having been offered something she could manage and that didn't come with the demands and stresses she had almost become used to. Stress was of course a part of her work experience. But now there was hope it would be significantly reduced. And that's exactly what she had wanted and needed. Once again there seemed little doubt God had His hand in all of this. There were in fact so many things that could have gotten in the way; things that would have made a change so terribly difficult and stressful. She surely would have experienced a high level of anxiety when starting her search for a way out of her old profiled career. But amazingly barriers were pushed aside, and she was given a new job within the company and was in some ways surprised at the ease with which it unfolded - and all to her benefit.

For Carol the way had been made clear only by her turning once again to The Shepherd and His promise. Even with the additional stress she had to deal with, she was always aware God was in control. While walking on the path she had been shown, her own faith was deepened from what she had come to understand. She was faced with the beautiful reality of seeing; knowing she was in His will, and that there really was a greater purpose to her illness, and to the trials she had to face. Slowly it was being revealed. And the comfort she felt helped sustain her through the continuing struggle. Without the hand of God touching her life and guiding her, she knew in her heart she would never have had the strength to go on. She knew it well, and it inspired her through the coming days, weeks and months. She would take each step with resolve and determination, leaning on Him when the going seemed insurmountable. And at times it certainly was.

It was one week after the offer that Robert, her own manager sent her the full details of the position they had discussed, including the recommended salary. He asked simply if she would review the offer and confirm her acceptance in writing. After looking carefully over the duties that were involved, she quickly realized she would have no difficulty at all performing any of them. It would have been a most satisfying opportunity for her after the ordeal she had moved through. And the only real learning curve would be mastering new software programs she was not familiar with. None of it seemed to suggest any undue stress or unseen pressures, and with it would come considerably less pressure as a result. And there was yet another benefit that she couldn't possibly have imagined: the salary which she anticipated would be cut by about a half was only reduced by 15%, actually holding her new salary well above the maximum allowed for that position. The reasons given were her considerable experience, years of service to the company and her education. Also a fact was she had contributed significantly to the companies last two mergers. She felt overwhelmed by his generous offer and by the recognition he gave for her outstanding work and dedication. Within a month she found herself in her new position, and we can only envision the feelings of relief after the despair she was facing in other areas of her life. But this move provided in many ways the first step up a new ladder where Hope could be stretched and experienced - and where dreams could become a possibility once more. In the quiet moments of the day she would see clearly the part God had played in her life. And would continue to play. All that had happened and unfolded to benefit her and her husband were not simply coincidence. In her obedience to Him, he had kept His promise and was lifting her out of the wilderness she had found herself in. There would be even more rejoicing ahead.

Chapter Twenty-One

THE FACE OF DESPAIR

CAROL HAD BEEN IN HER NEW JOB for only a month when she started to develop head tremors. It was emotionally crippling, and perhaps the most disturbing of all relapses because it was so noticeable to everyone around. Until this appeared, the symptoms had not been so obvious or distressing, and there was no way of hiding it. Her head shook constantly from left to right much like someone with Parkinson's might experience. It meant she was again unable to work because there was no possible way she could focus on her computer screen; a job that required eight hours a day of concentration along with the necessary written work. There was not even the remotest chance of her being able to do it. It was a devastating time for her. It seemed she was being beaten back yet again by what had taken-over her life with the diagnosis.

She took the only step she could by seeking treatment from the MS clinic where they suggested the disease had likely progressed to include yet another auto-immune disorder such as Parkinson's. The thought of continuing-on with so much against her was overwhelming. The possibility of having to live with the uncontrollable shaking was becoming more real than she ever imagined, and she knew it could slowly progress into her hands and feet. The tremors had already become almost painful, and everything she attempted was challenged by the shaking she was experiencing. Even the simple task of sitting in church to hear the message was extraordinarily difficult because of the tremors, and naturally she was self-conscious of what it might look like to those around her. On a daily, even hourly basis she was faced with every ordinary chore where she would be put to the test. There would be the simple, almost expected freedom of climbing into the car and heading for a store; trying to focus on essential family needs and even the effort and concentration needed with basic expectations around the home. Soon however, even the freedom to drive was taken away.

We can only speculate on the emotions when she, and they as a couple would sit at the table for dinner. We naturally think of where the conversation might go, and where the thoughts would really have been. Certainly not so much on the pleasure of enjoying a good meal, as much as they would have tried. But every effort was made to continue their lives as they had in the past; to let things be as normal as they could possibly be under the circumstances. However, some of the things taken for granted now became an impediment that was at times overpowering. Little things would challenge every moment of the day, leaving her consumed with the hopelessness that would have her question the reason for going-on. Was it all worth it in the end? Of course she was always aware of the part God was playing in her life, but in the raw vulnerability of our humanity we will at times fall into despair and question our very existence. In such a position as she was in, we would all look for the reasons why. And most of us, if honest would be stifled by the silence of our fear. The anxiety and uncertainty would quickly begin to direct our thoughts, along with whatever energy remained. She knew there was no way of stopping the onslaught she struggled with, and she must have felt all too often the insufferable pain and torment beyond anything she could have imagined. Everything seemed to be going the wrong way after that incredible opportunity of being handed a new position. How could she possibly survive the pressures and stresses she was under.

In the few moments she could claim as her own, she continued to think of seeking salvation for her husband, asking God to save him. She would pray for this even in the midst of her illness for she herself had come to see and understand above and beyond the temporal challenges of this life here on earth, there was a peace; an eternity without end. No matter what she was tested with in this life, it would one day fade, and nothing compared to what God had promised and prepared for those who loved Him. It was unbearable to think of Dave not being saved. And it was this that was still foremost in her mind.

Since Carol had joined the church and changed her very life, her husband, although not following in her footsteps never questioned her commitment nor the time she gave to her belief and desire to follow Jesus. But there would be times when she struggled with thoughts over the issues which put an occasional strain on their relationship. They would talk and share thoughts; perceptions about faith and God - and even attitudes and perspectives which over the years demanded attention. But in the end, there was between them an understanding - even though in some ways they held different views. Dave was a wonderful husband; loyal and deeply caring, and he supported his wife even though perhaps spiritually at least, and for the moment they walked a different path. But there was another reality to it all. And she embraced the scriptures which gave guidance and understanding to their togetherness. She loved him dearly, and he, her. And in this meeting of shared affection and love she was able to better understand the meaning of Paul's words in First Corinthians 7:12-14:

> *"But to the rest speak I, not the Lord: If any brother hath a wife that believeth not, and she be pleased to dwell with him, let him not put her away.*
> *13 And the woman which hath an husband that believeth not, and if he be pleased to dwell with her, let her not leave him.*
> *14 For the unbelieving husband is <u>sanctified</u> by the wife, and the unbelieving wife is <u>sanctified</u> by the husband: else were your children unclean; but now are they holy."*

The word "**sanctified**" literally means to make holy. And so, a marriage where even spiritual differences are evident is blessed when they are united with love and mutual respect. In fact, it is the will of the Lord that they be together. Carol then continued to pray that God would use whatever circumstances were necessary to bring her husband to repentance, with a desire to know Him as she herself did. She would pray he would seek His very face in Forgiveness, and left it at His feet in the hope of his salvation.

At this time of their lives anyway, and on a daily basis she worked to conceal her despair over her condition from Dave. Then one evening at home her containment burst from the pressure of her struggle to go-on. After shaking uncontrollably while trying to read, she lifted herself out of the Lazy Boy and somehow made her way to the dining room where she could be alone with her grief and pain. It seemed all that had in the past brought her pleasure was being taken. Now she could barely read. She'd already given up the opportunity and joy of being around her horses for the stamina simply was no longer there. She had stopped riding and no longer had the horse that had meant so much to her. She even walked and moved with great caution because of the numbness in her feet. It would all influence her sense of security with even the most basic tasks - things we all take for granted. She was unsure of her footing when walking or climbing a stair, and she found herself in such pain. Slowly, her ability to function as she had in the past was slipping away. But she continued in her trust of God, no matter the loss of strength in her body. Understandably, it was almost impossible to cover-up the reality from her husband, as much as she tried.

She had retreated to the dining room to spare Dave the distress she was experiencing. Surely all hope must have left her at that moment. She wept uncontrollably, holding her head in her hands, pleading for it all to stop. She could take it no longer. But it wasn't long before Dave came into the room and saw her dreadful debilitating condition. She was spent; hopelessly overwhelmed with all she was facing, and the future was slowly being erased from her thoughts. Dave held his wife as she wept in complete desperation. He didn't speak for he knew words at this time were of little value. He just held her as she sobbed her grief, letting it spill out of her into a pool of painful reality. But what she couldn't have expected was his next move after seeing his beloved wife so hurt. And more than anything perhaps it showed the depth of his love for her. The disease which had robbed them of so much was seemingly giving back even more. And now her own love for him was sealed as she saw his attempts to help in any way he could as the illness had progressed.

That night she turned-in to bed not knowing her husband would spend the night searching the internet for answers. He was determined; resolute to find a way to give hope to his wife and to their future together. In the early hours of the following morning he walked into the bedroom excited with something he had found. Waving three pages of his research, he said calmly, "I think I've found the answer. I know now where I'm going to send you."

He had in fact found the Sanoviv Medical Institute in Mexico; a remarkable facility that deals with alternative and holistic integrative medicine, focusing on cutting edge diagnostics, nutrition and detoxifying while avoiding the use of drugs unless absolutely necessary. It sounded too good to be true. But there it was.

As she read the pages given to her, she wondered if this was God's answer to her prayers. Patiently, Dave waited for a response. Understandably she was uncertain and needed more time to think it through. She again went into prayer, handing-over the difficulty of deciding to Christ. She was in reality becoming too weak to struggle in her search for answers. Soon there was a change that came with it's own special comfort. There appeared in her heart and mind a sense of peace which flowed through her, and it wasn't long before they began to make plans to get her to the hospital in Rosarito, Mexico; the Sanoviv Medical Institute. In a preceding dialogue with them they gave reassurance that while they could not promise to cure the disease (there was no cure) they may be able to halt it's progression and perhaps even reverse the current impacts of it on her body. Being outside of Canada, there was no coverage to help with the enormous cost of the treatment, and unfortunately she was not able to receive compensation from her private insurance either. It was a tremendous blow to them as they considered every option; every possibility.

Regardless of the cost, together they decided it was the right thing to do and they took on the challenge of meeting the financial burden in other ways. It would be difficult beyond belief, and everything - including her life was at stake. It would have been a terrifying thought once they had decided on the treatment. Now they had to find ways to make it work. Every penny of it would be out of their own pockets, and after all that had happened to them, those pockets were not deep by any standard. Still, she felt at peace with what they had decided on, and as quickly as they could, they made travel plans to leave Canada for a three week initial stay at the center in Mexico. She wasn't scheduled to return to work until November. It was now late August, 2009 and so she could to some extent relax with the thought there was a good window to commit herself to the hands of others, now in a foreign medical facility and with professionals she didn't know. In fact she was scheduled to check-in on September 19, 2009; a moment she would be thinking about every minute of the day. But there was another reality she wasn't aware of at the time: the decision they had made, and the trust she had extended to this unknown venture would in the end change both of their lives in ways she couldn't have dreamed of. Even before arriving she had been enrolled in the Neuro-Repair program tailored specifically to patients who were suffering from MS.

At this moment in her journey, she knew there was no other hope because the treatments she had undergone in Canada and the drugs prescribed had given her no relief - and no hope for the future. In fact, she was getting worse as the days went by, and each relapse came with even greater disabling effects and longer absences from work. She was desperate for answers, and the decision to leave the country for help was the only thing left that gave her any sense of hope. Through the endless hours of anguish as she waited, she did the best she could and tried above all else to leave it in the hands of God himself. There was simply nothing else she could do. Finally, with arrangements made and the flight booked, she was soon on her way to Sanoviv, and the promise of a new tomorrow.

Chapter Twenty-Two

THE MIRACLE AT SANOVIV

BEING ACCUSTOMED TO THE ENVIRONMENT OF A typical Canadian hospital, Carol was completely unprepared for what she found at the medical institute in Mexico. The times in her home country when hospitalized had been particularly stressful, leaving her with minimal hope. Attention to her condition seemed rationed at best, and basic encouragement was simply absent. She was given few answers to her questions and the whole process, each time tended toward the mechanical, leaving little time for the comfort of the human touch along with an understanding of her condition. Missing also was any sense of interest, and she felt little more than a number on an assembly line already choked with others also in desperate need.

In her experience, it seemed only the symptoms were being treated rather than the underlying cause. And that's exactly how it appeared to a patient facing a possible life and death situation. Solutions to her problem were expressed through the drugs they would try on top of what she was already taking for MS. Given her new symptoms, they wanted to layer medication designed for Parkinson's Disease to deal with the head tremors she was experiencing. But along with her husband, they decided against this approach no-doubt feeling the treatment was guess-work at best, and in fact could be harmful over the long term. They had researched carefully the problems with Multiple Sclerosis, realizing of course there had to be an underlying cause which needed to be addressed. They were seeking not only help and direction, but also an understandingof what was really happening to her body. The doctors did look for what was causing it to virtually attack itself, as if thinking it was harboring a foreign matter, yet the findings of their search seemed unclear. Surely on some level they must have been aware whatever the reason for the attack, it was causing the myelin sheath covering the nerves transmitting signals to be stripped away, resulting in an apparent short-circuit to the system. In other words the signals leaving the brain were not reaching their intended destination. In the simplest way, that's what appeared to be happening. In the end, Carol and Dave were left feeling out in the cold while being pressured to accept a treatment they themselves seemed unsure of. It was all so discouraging - and frightening. Did anyone anywhere have the answers?

The day Carol arrived by herself in San Diego California, there was a shuttle-bus from the hospital waiting for her at the airport. From there it would take her into Mexico and ultimately to the town of Rosarito where the institute was. There was no need to look for transportation or even think of taking the next step alone. Everything had been taken-care-of which she found comforting given the stress she was under. It was the perfect touch for Carol arriving in a strange city while dealing not only physically but also emotionally with the weight of her diagnosis. That was a natural worry she carried deep inside, hiding the feelings at times even from herself. There had to be considerable apprehension given her circumstances and thoughts about the past experiences with another medical community where progress was little more than a distant dream. Once at the institute however she would have also been filled with questions and yet eager to get-on with the task at hand. This was altogether a new opportunity to feel at least some encouragement given all she had read about the facility. With her mind full of thoughts, her family and home, she would turn frequently to God for her comfort. Staying with her faith was crucial as she found herself preparing mentally for a new approach to her dilemma.

Interestingly, there was an encouraging and unexpected surprise once her bus had almost reached its destination. As they motored-on, the drive took them past a site she would remember for the rest of her life. Turning to glance out the window, she was taken with the image that came into view. Looking-up, her eyes became fixed on the magnificent seventy-five foot statue of Jesus - "Christ of The Sacred Heart". It was at once inspiring and she leapt with joy at the sight of it, His arms outstretched as if to welcome her; to love and protect her through her time there. It was a wonderful beginning to her arrival at the hospital and filled her with comfort and hope.

Carol was scheduled to be in Sanoviv for three weeks, but with an unplanned surgery now being a part of the plan, she would be there for four. The regimen would do justice to any military protocol on any continent. Each day started at 6:00 A.M.

and every minute of the day was filled with testing and checking the patient until around 8:00 P.M. in the evening. It was extremely rigorous with every activity and event carefully planned and deliberately orchestrated. She couldn't help but be impressed with their efficiency and as soon as she could she shared her feelings with Dave who was anxiously waiting at home for any news.

Each morning began with either meditation or yoga, followed as the day unfolded in meetings with various physicians and other health professionals. Then there were the endless tests and treatments, concluding a lecture designed to educate the patient on numerous health concerns, lifestyles and nutrition. This remarkable institute treated the whole person, mind, body and spirit, and not just a specific disorder, and would include working with, in Carol's case a neurologist, dentist, chiropractor, nutritionist, fitness experts and therapists, including of course a medical doctor and even a psychologist. She would meet with each daily for the first week while intensive testing was being done. No stone was left unturned to determine if other factors were affecting her health. They would check and double check her condition including blood, stool, urine and skin. There would be thermography which allows specialists to see variations in body temperature (Excellent for indicating the presence of allergies) and X-rays, ultrasound and so many others. They couldn't have been more thorough in their effort to find-out all that was going-on with Carol.

To help in their work, the entire place; the building and the environment she was in was totally free of any toxins, and all the food prepared was entirely organic. Anything considered potentially harmful such as coffee, gluten, alcohol and red meat were simply not allowed. It was in effect an environment designed to maximize the success of the patient's stay; to determine the root cause of any disorder they might find, and to promote a healthy recovery. For Carol dealing with MS this was crucial, and she quickly gained confidence in her new surroundings, feeling they had her best interests at heart. And there was no question they did. Finally she could begin to trust in her health care once again, and she was greatly encouraged by the care and attention she was given.

When Carol first arrived at the facility her medical condition was very poor. Not only had the relapses along with the medications ravaged her physically and mentally, she suffered severe insomnia which left her exhausted. The fatigue was almost disabling, especially during the hot summer months, and she struggled with not only the head tremors, but also with continued numbness in her feet. Before going to the institute in Mexico she'd already started the process of removing amalgam fillings (containing mercury) from her teeth because it had been suggested there could be a possible link to Multiple Sclerosis. There were also some risks associated with common root canals that could cause infection throughout the body. This has been a bone of contention amongst many professionals in the field, but for those with a particular interest, they might consider reading the work of Dr. Weston A. Price from over a century ago. The results of his own research and all he contributed to our understanding of that particular problem are startling. More recent studies have confirmed his findings, but numerous professional organizations such as the ADA continue to insist on the safety of the procedure. While the issues are complicated and lengthy, it's encouraging to know many in the medical community are paying attention to what has been uncovered to this point.

As treatments got underway at the Sanoviv institute, Carol was starting to feel a slight difference to the pain in her legs. Slowly it began to lessen, and to her surprise, the head tremors also were beginning to decrease. For the very first time since being diagnosed with MS her health seemed to be taking an upward turn, and all without the use of drugs. Before arriving at Sanoviv she had stopped taking the MS injections prescribed because she didn't want anything to interfere with the new treatment she would be getting, and that seemed to hold so much promise. Now, as each day passed at the institute, she was feeling more reassured. And, just as they had promised, it wasn't long before they were having success reversing some of the symptoms she had arrived with. We can only imagine her feelings after what she had gone through those months before this experience. At last now there was hope.

After the long days of assessment and treatment, and into the evening, patients at the institute were invited to attend lectures and discussions about health issues and lifestyles. Through these opportunities Carol learned about the dietary and related lifestyle changes she would have to make once back in her home in Canada. If she expected lasting effects in curbing the progression of MS she would have to maintain a particular focus on what she would eat while thinking back on her experience at the hospital. There was much to remember, and she now realized the significance of staying on track with proper foods, rest and even exercise. On top of that were thoughts of issues covered with the psychologist - all of which influence one's health in one way or another.

Over the days before leaving the hospital she was noticing slight changes in her condition, the hours bringing measurable moments of relief. Perhaps there were times she would question her thoughts, given the prognosis offered by doctors in her home town two countries away. Then during the final week of her stay, keeping in mind the high level of communication the medical staff exercised, they shared with her the very real possibility of yet another auto-immune disease she could be struggling with: Celiac. Celiac disease is first and foremost an auto-immune disorder that results in damage to the lining of the small intestine when foods containing gluten are consumed. Gluten is a protein found in many grains whose damage to the intestine makes it difficult for the system to absorb nutrients from the food - especially fat, calcium, iron and folate. One can only speculate on the thoughts that ran through her head upon hearing this after all she had gone through. She must have been stunned; certainly bewildered hearing those words. What else could possibly go wrong? She would have had so many questions looking for an answer. And how would Dave, her husband take the news, knowing how sick his wife had been.

After a little extra research and questions for her medical team, that evening she shared the news with him. His heart sank at the thought of her having yet another devastating disease. When she responded, saying it was perhaps a good thing, he couldn't begin to understand what she was suggesting. She imagined his face when the phone went silent. But after a while she was able to explain her thinking, outlining just what Celiac was and how the presence of gluten in her diet may well have been responsible for triggering the relapses she suffered. In simple terms it meant that if gluten could be avoided, it could greatly reduce the number and even the severity of her relapses which were believed to be the result of her diagnosed Multiple Sclerosis.

It seemed Dave was starting to see what she was saying. From his response she knew he was also seeing the sun breaking through the clouds, and it lifted her heart. She well knew the effect all this had on him as he kept the home fires burning, waiting for her return. Still, the possibility of Celiac hadn't been confirmed through actual testing. That wouldn't happen for another quarter of a year. Regardless, judging by the progress she had made since being at Sanoviv and on a gluten-free diet, it was looking more and more likely. The fact remained, it takes up to six months for the intestinal tract to heal after eliminating gluten from the diet. And really, only then would they be able to fully see the impact gluten had made on her.

The time finally came when she would return home to Canada. The experience at Sanoviv had been nothing short of a miracle. Her overall health was improving daily and noticeably filling her with hope and a welcomed reassurance. Once back however, the panic set-in when she realized all that had to be overcome daily to maintain her health and the new lifestyle.

Thoughts plagued her with how she could work her diet in the 'real-world' where there were no trained chefs to prepare her food or monitor her activities in the kitchen. How could she even begin to cope with all the changes needed to ensure her progress? She was no longer secluded or protected from the world of toxins, and how she could hope to handle the challenges of a gluten-free diet was beyond her. At least for the moment.

One of the biggest problems faced was not just maintaining a totally gluten-free home, but also the very real possibility of contamination. The minutest trace of gluten is sufficient to prevent a full recovery from the disease. In fact, an amount equivalent to one sixteenth of a finger-nail would be enough to keep you sick. And it promised to be an unbelievable challenge as Dave would still be eatinga normal diet. Toasters and work surfaces in the kitchen used to prepare food couldn't be shared. For her, it had to be completely gluten free. Her husband, lovingly knowing how difficult or impossible this could be made a decision: he too would be totally gluten-free to help his wife. It was an incredible commitment, and an act of pure love.

Unbeknown to her, before she returned home he had taken steps to clear the kitchen of any products containing gluten. The cupboards, fridge and freezer were emptied, cleared and cleaned to ensure as sterile an environment as possible. Only fruit, vegetables, meat, dairy products and fish were left. The rest had gone. Their new diet would consist of vegetables, fruit and fish for the most part. Together they chose to also eliminate beef, pork and dairy products based on what she had learned from the lectures back at the institute. The effects of these foods were particularly harmful, especially to someone recuperating from Celiac - if indeed she had that disease! Although it would be an incredible challenge, if they could do it, it would mean improved health possibly for both of them. But certainly for Carol. Amongst other things, they had to find a local farmer that sold fresh organic vegetables. There simply wasn't nearly enough variety in the local grocery stores to provide a balanced diet. And most of the foods there anyway would not be organic; free from pesticides etc. In organic farming, synthetic pesticides and chemical fertilizers are not allowed, and the very soil in which the crops are grown, is by comparison more pristine and robust.

Given the Canadian climate too, many of the vegetables needed would be available only in the summer months. Foods that are shipped across country lose their nutritional properties fairly quickly over time and do little to feed a body in need of a healthy diet that is nutritionally rich. Carol's body had been so depleted and had been, amongst other problems, showing signs of MS. At least, the new approach to eating better would or could offer hope for this too, along with a regimen of high quality vitamins that came with a heavy tab themselves. They chose to use Usana which is a pharmaceutical grade of vitamins with a far superior quality over those offered at the local store. In fact there was no comparison once they researched them all. But it would again hit the wallet hard. Along with the cost of the hospital in Mexico, a gluten-free organic diet and vitamins, their financial position was quickly changing. They had no choice but to continue using their line of credit to pay for her stay at the institute, and their combined salaries would be used to try to maintain the new lifestyle. In looking at the big picture, Carol would continue to put her trust in God that this was the answer they were looking for. And in all truth, there was in fact nothing else she could do.

"Commit your way to The Lord; trust in Him and He will act."
Psalm 37:5

Chapter Twenty-Three

GOD'S WILL, NOT MINE

ANOTHER SURPRISE AWAITED CAROL ONCE SHE ARRIVED home. There was a news release describing a treatment for MS which appeared to be healing many patients struggling with it. Some of those previously in wheelchairs were beginning to walk again and there were numerous testimonies of improved health generally. The procedure was directly related to a condition called Chronic Cerebrospinal Venous Insufficiency or CCSVI which describes a compromised blood flow in the veins draining the central nervous system. It involves the veins in the head and neck which may be narrowed or at least blocked, and naturally unable to efficiently remove blood from that system. The Italian physician who developed this theory and brought it to life in 2008 was Paolo Zamboni from the University of Ferrara.

Encouraged by his own research, he hypothesized it may well play a role in healing or even in the development of Multiple Sclerosis. He went on to devise a treatment he called 'liberation therapy' which involved venoplasty (or stenting) of particular veins to improve blood flow and included balloon angioplasty as an alternative treatment (or an added one) for patients suffering from MS. Regardless of conflicting opinions in the medical community, it gave so many victims of this dreaded and incurable disease a sense of hope in the progress that had been reported. At its introduction there was promise for patients of a new freedom and a more encouraging future if everything went according to plan. It was an exciting possibility; the news spreading quickly from one continent to another. At last, it seemed the scene and even the expectations might be changing for so many of the suffering victims. There really was a light at the end of the tunnel. For Carol, naturally there were thoughts she could at last see the reversal of the effects of the disease, and a hopeful reduction in relapses through the gluten-free diet as well - if in fact she did also have the Celiac condition. Still, after returning home, and after all she had gone through, she found it all so challenging.

It wasn't long before she returned to work, but now she would arrive home in the early evening still feeling drained; exhausted, with little or no energy left to take-on the other things she needed to do. The strength needed even in preparing meals was too much, never failing to remind her that fatigue on this level was one of the most prevalent symptoms of Multiple Sclerosis. Thinking once more of the news she had heard, she too was encouraged; her hopes being high that the procedure, if it really did work, might provide her with the energy needed to go-on. She somehow felt deep down inside she might regain the level she had known just a short while ago, before all of this had fallen-in on her. Again, only time would tell.

The procedure she needed was only available in Italy at the time. The neurologist there at the center was already treating patients - and with success. In fact, one of them happened to be his own wife. The very thought of it lifted her spirits. Now being determined to sign-up for the treatment when possible, she again contacted the institute at Sanoviv to see if they themselves had been involved in the new process, and if so, would they be offering the treatment in the future as part of their neurological program? As it happened they were already in the process of sending one of their surgeons to Italy to work with Dr. Zamboni and his team to learn the technique first hand, and to master the necessary surgical procedure.

Within a year Carol had made plans to return to Sanoviv to have the tests done and to see if she was in fact eligible for the program. Essentially it consisted of a simple ultrasound which would confirm a blockage of one of the arteries. Perhaps even both. If a blockage was found, there was no doubt she'd be approved for the procedure. Unfortunately, it wasn't available in Canada, and still isn't at the time of this writing. Consequently, if she was in fact a candidate, it would have to be done again in Mexico, in a little town close to the sea - and where miracles don't seem so uncommon anymore. Still, they had to take into consideration the added cost of the treatment and another visit to the institute. To be accepted on the CCSVI program would be an additional $25,000 - and that's on top of the $35,000 her stay there had already cost. One really has to wonder at the power of Faith on a journey such as this.

When she returned to Sanoviv for the second time, her husband Dave was with her. While Carol's other condition of possible Celiac disease hadn't yet been confirmed, (at this point she had been diagnosed only with MS) she had remained on the gluten-free diet along with her husband. Over time they noticed his pain level and other symptoms had lessened while following that same regimen. Surely there must be some connection. As a result, they decided to go together to the institute, for he was also dealing with hypothyroidism, a goiter and Lyme's Disease. They both believed with all their hearts he would benefit by going through their diagnostic program which meant a stay of at least a week. But they couldn't escape the thought that this program alone would cost another $15,000. Now they would have a total of $75,000 on their line of credit to handle at some time in the future. In fact they had come to realize when all was done, they would simply have to re-finance the house and add it to the existing mortgage.

Once at the institute, Dave was also put through a series of tests to diagnose every medical problem he might have been dealing with. It was again extensive and thorough, leaving nothing to chance. After a while it was confirmed that he too had an intolerance to gluten, which explained why his pain had lessened over the year on their gluten-free diet. Still, with his vitamin and mineral levels so depleted, the specialists working on his case recommended a treatment that involved removing several vials of blood in order to restore the cells to optimum condition. Later they would be re-introduced into the body through daily injections over a thirty day period, filling his system with strong healthy cells to encourage optimum health.

This procedure, called plasmapheresis is particularly successful in conditions we find under autoimmune diseases. It effectively removes auto-antibodies from the blood. These are immune proteins (antibodies) that mistakenly target an individual's own tissues or organs. In other words they lose their ability to distinguish whatever may threaten the system, sometimes attacking 'self ' as if perceiving an invasion of a foreign substance such as a virus or bacteria. The body produces antibodies to defend itself, and in these cases, where they are not able to discriminate between 'self ' or 'non-self ' they result in auto-antibodies which ultimately can cause inflammation, damage to organs and even entire systems, leading to their eventual dysfunction.

There was in fact an added problem that went along with the procedure. The daily injections Dave needed where cells were reintroduced back into the body came with its own set of unexpected problems. With the original cost already impacting heavily on them financially, there appeared a further burden from the procedure. Because the suspensions could not be delivered over the border into Canada, it meant they would have to pay the extra expense of another visit to Sanoviv to pick them up personally. But in the end it worked-out well. And whatever the cost of all that had to be done, it was more than worth it. Can anyone really but a price on the cost of one's health? Is any amount really too much? I think the answer is clear.

While her husband was going through the process described at the institute, Carol herself was being tested for CCSVI as originally planned. In fact, she was the first patient at that facility to go through it, and basically they were still learning the ropes so to speak. To actually qualify for it, the blockage of veins needed to be in excess of 50%. Unfortunately, as it happened, she didn't qualify for the procedure because her blockages were less. She was naturally disappointed as she'd hoped it would clear-up so many of her concerns, including her extreme fatigue, which was the one lasting symptom resulting from her MS.

Three months had passed before they returned to the center to pick-up the vials of blood for Dave, and once again together they went through yet another diagnostic program as a cost of almost yet another $15,000. At that time, and to her complete surprise, the doctor assigned to her explained that in her earlier visit, they had failed to perform the ultrasound properly. It turned-out Carol should have been sitting-up for the test, and not laying down, and they wanted her to re-do it. Such an invitation brought her great relief and enormous encouragement. What if, this time they found the blockage and cleared it? What if it worked and she could return home free from all the symptoms she had struggled with as a woman living with Multiple Sclerosis?

The test was completed, and this time the results were totally different. The vein on the right side of her neck was 75% blocked, while that on the left side was showing a blockage of 100%. Incredible. Without reservation it qualified her for the treatment of CCSVI and it was quickly scheduled over the following two days. The neurologist wanted to perform an MRI of the neck and brain prior to the procedure. The findings were remarkable. The MRI showed that the several lesions on her brain were completely healed, and around the blocked vein in her neck three smaller veins had developed to help deal with the flow of blood. But of course, in reality that was not nearly adequate to deal with the situation that had become very serious. The procedure Carol was prepared for involved a balloon angioplasty which is designed to clear blockages of blood flow in chest and neck veins. The attending physician prefers the patient be fully awake and aware before starting. Once the skin and tissue around the groin are slightly anesthetized, a small needle is used to puncture the femoral vein. A guide-wire is pushed through the needle into the vein and the needle is removed, being replaced with a catheter introduced over the wire. It's then threaded up into the right ventricle of the heart and out of the right atrium into the superior vena cava. From there, the doctor can access the veins that drain the central nervous system, including the jugular vein and others. In balloon angioplasty, a vein is opened or widened by inflating a small balloon for a short period of time. In fact it may be inflated a number of times to ensure a blockage has been cleared. Once done, the catheter is slowly pulled back out of the body, often while being viewed by the patient herself. This is exactly what Carol did, watching the entire procedure on a nearby screen. For most of us, it would be a sight we would choose to avoid. But not this young woman. It was in fact all too exciting to miss.

The procedure was a great success, although it would be a couple of weeks before she would actually know and feel the difference after returning home. Dave also could revel in the improvement in his own health. For reasons still unknown, most of his health issues were not diagnosed in his own country, even after all the testing he was subjected to. His thyroid problem though had been brought to light, but he chose not to pursue treatment in Canada because their plan was simply to remove it, which would result in a lifetime of drugs to replace the hormones effecting metabolism as well as cholesterol levels. He was very familiar with the difficulties faced if this were to happen because not only his mother, but also his two brothers had already had their thyroids removed.

As a family, they had all been affected with thyroid problems and more than likely he was genetically predisposed for that condition. While iodine deficiency worldwide is linked to hypothyroidism, in North America this is usually not a problem, and the condition then was most likely connected to a hereditary disease such as Hashimoto's Thyroiditis. Dave's thyroid though was still registering at least a degree of functioning and he'd been treating it with herbal therapy and related remedies. On their return to Canada they'd been fortunate in locating a superb herbalist who continued to test him every three months to confirm his progress through herbal use. At a later time, he was also introduced to, and used an Avatar machine which turned-out to be incredibly helpful for this and other concerns he'd been dealing with over the years. Things had improved dramatically then for both of them, and finally the future at least in terms of their health was looking so very good. Clearly the cost of their involvement with an out-of-country facility had been more than worth it. In truth, together, they had never felt so good. The challenge now was to maintain the effort and not slip into any habit that might compromise their progress.

It's at this point there is yet another reality which must be brought into focus. Over a considerable period of time, Carol's struggles had been nothing short of horrendous. We can only imagine the emotions she dealt with through her trials; the questioning and the fear. It would have been overwhelming, and I can only admire her tremendous courage through it all.

In a meeting with her neurologist at the institute before returning home, she sat with her husband by her side while he discussed her condition; her treatments and her progress. In front of him were the charts; reports, X-rays and MRI relating to her stay there and other details she may not have been aware of at the time. But most of the words coming from him were in Spanish and she couldn't understand. By his side was a nurse who translated her thoughts and questions, and any concerns she was feeling. Then toward the end of this special conference, and looking at both of them as they sat with understandable apprehension, he asked why she had come to Sanoviv in the first place. His nurse translated his questions and Carol must have raised an eyebrow at what she surely would have considered his rather curious query. It was MS.

There was a moment of silence as he looked across the desk and into her face. After what seemed like a lifetime of waiting, he finally spoke - "Carol - the truth is, you don't have MS." he said, carefully choosing his words. "In fact, you never did. The lesions on your brain that had been seen were caused by Celiac disease - not Multiple Sclerosis. It's something we suspected for a while as you know, but we wanted to be sure before we told you."

Deeply relieved at the news, they were both somewhat stunned; even overwhelmed by it all after going through so much. Was there really a chance at a perfectly normal life after all that had happened to her - and to them as a couple? She made a comment to the physician behind the desk and found herself first glancing over at Dave and then automatically pushing herself out of the chair. Turning to thank him, they walked out of the office and into the hall where they simply stood and looked at each-other for a moment. The feelings they would have entertained are not difficult to imagine. In fact, perhaps at this time in their journey that's all they were left with; feelings. There really was little else to say after getting such news.

"Well, I'm clear of the symptoms, except for some fatigue," she said, looking into Dave's face, almost in disbelief. "I still have to deal with the Celiac Disease though, but with help, I know we can do it." He nodded, knowing the full significance it was going to make in their lives. Now they could move forward, and into a new beginning.

Soon her old energy levels would return and she would once more know the joy and freedom of fully functioning again; of being complete - just as she had before the drama took over her existence. It was as if her very life had been given back to her; a gift of the girl she had been before. And indeed, a gift it was. A gift from God himself. The relief would have been palpable; earth-shaking after all she had suffered through. They held each-other tightly for a while longer, filled with the sense of being delivered from a sentence that threatened to destroy her and all they had hoped for as a husband

and wife. And their tears flowed freely until a certain peace settled into their thoughts. Until they were still.

There was much for them to think on after their ordeals over those many months with health scares and the like. But the end result of their thoughts, for Carol were relatively simple. She knew God's hand had directed their lives in ways that she perhaps couldn't have imagined just a few years before. For one thing, if they had not sought treatment in Sanoviv, tragically, the medical teams in her own country would have continued treating a disease she didn't have with drug therapy, the side effects of which can be calamitous. It may well have impacted other organs as time went on. And because they had not been treating the real issues she was dealing with, her health would have steadily deteriorated over the months, eventually leaving her in a state that was too horrendous to even think about. The Celiac Disease would have remained untreated and her body would have been the relentless victim of malnutrition over a short period of time. In turn she would have not been able to work, and their combined dreams and hopes as a couple would never have been realized.

The state of Dave's health also would have continued to deteriorate because of his own gluten intolerance as well as the thyroid difficulty and Lyme's Disease. It was exhausting him. His job required great physical stamina and his health condition, before getting the attention he needed was quickly being reduced to the point of barely surviving. The pain he struggled with was never-ending, and his occupation demanded so much of his mind and body. It would have been hard if not impossible to maintain the strength and the sheer effort had the problems not been treated as they were. In the end, they carried a cost of almost $100,000 for the treatments received. Staggering in itself. But they knew they had been blessed beyond words.

As for Carol, she had thankfully left her management position and acquired a less stressful job where she could be home in the evenings with her husband and pursue her special spiritual interests. The opportunity it gave them couldn't really be described. But there is a particular point she wanted to make as her story unfolded over the hours and the days I sat with her. Her tale is heroic. Beautiful. Deeply encouraging and filled with hope. And I remember the long pause as I looked across the wooden table into her eyes. I waited patiently for the pieces I knew she was using to tie-up the informal minutes of this very personal journal in the only way she could; with an unvarnished truth that had been earned on the battlefield of Life by a child of God. This then was her story: and as time went by she came to understand had she never been diagnosed with MS in the first place, she never would have gone to Sanoviv where she learned so very much about creating a healthier lifestyle. Dave would never have known the real issues associated with his own health. And she may never have known the reality of her own condition that was slowly destroying her.

Spiritually, the real significance is even greater: from her diagnosis came numerous blessings that were from no other source but God. It got her attention, and that of her husband and gave the whole experience a new kind of meaning. An unexpected purpose if you like. Dave was better able to understand how her faith and a life devoted to God had positively affected his life in so many ways, and indeed their marriage. He also realized how his own health finally had been turned around for the better through the experiences Carol had been forced into taking. It was remarkable in the extreme, and she would reflect on the scripture.

"*The goodness of God shall draw men unto repentance.*"

Earlier you will remember, Carol was delivered from the grasp of alcohol and looking back, her illness and related circumstances brought about the healing of her husband. It was all becoming clear now. At the time of writing, they have been together for over 28 years and married for more than seventeen of them. Their marriage improved, as did their overall relationship, enriching it; making it more wonderful than it had ever been in the past. Another blessing that was so needed. Without all she had experienced in her personal life as well as the health crisis she suffered, their marriage may well have ended in divorce. Her drinking would have eventually cost her her job because she'd already included that into her everyday activity even at work. Thanks to Dave and his effort to get the help she needed, she would have otherwise been at the mercy of the medical teams who didn't seem to pay further attention to her needs once she'd been diagnosed with MS. The result of it all, as the pieces of the puzzle fell into place, was her complete recovery from all she had been afflicted with. Without the happenings described, she quite likely would have been institutionalized because there would have been no way she could care for herself. A truly remarkable turn of events.

Were all these events following her decision to find and follow God those fifteen years ago a coincidence that simply played themselves out to the end? Not a chance. It was only because of God that she has such an abundant life today and a bright wonderfully exciting future - not only in this life, but in the life to come for all Eternity.

I shall never forget the look in her eyes when she spoke those final words at the end of our time together. For a moment she looked about the room where we had spent so many hours discussing her journey; as if to remind herself of something; something she was looking for - yet now something she had finally found. I noticed her glance at the pictures in the china cabinet and then again to the one behind her when she was just a young inquisitive girl of ten waiting for her future to unfold. I could see clearly the emotions she held as she turned back to face me.

"You know, after coming to know God, I really think my greatest gift is a wonderful husband that I came so close to losing. Looking back, if it had not been for that night; the night of February 15, 1999 when in desperation I fell to my knees and prayed, my life and my husband's would have been drastically different. Only God could have taken such a life as mine filled with bitterness, anger and unforgiveness and transformed it into what is now; a life filled with love and peace."

Without saying a word, she set a piece of paper down on the table and slid it toward me. I looked at her through the silence for a moment before picking it up. On it was written a poem, along with a date filled-in at the bottom of the page: "November 13, 2015." It was Carol's own poem which I was anxious to read after all I had come to know about her life, and so I have copied and placed it at the back of the book because of all that it holds. All that it tells. And all that it means, and it speaks for itself as you will see. The title is "Past, Present and Future".

We sat for a while in the silence of a journey that was finally understood with not a word being said. Then, lifting my pen from the paper I nodded my awareness of what she was feeling. In my heart I knew she had finally come home; come home to His love and forgiveness. And there was nothing else to say. The story was almost finished. Yet in the quiet of my mind, and with a heart full of respect for the Carol I had come to know, I couldn't help thinking on the words from Roman's 8:39 "*Nothing. Nothing in all creation is able to separate us from the love of God in Christ Jesus.*"

Chapter Twenty-Four

A BRIEF ENCOUNTER

HAPPINESS IS A WONDERFUL THING. IT MAY be fleeting, or hang around for long stretches of Time. But it's something we embrace and enjoy at the moment and occasionally for generous lengths of our biography. Still, it's something we experience in the 'now'. It's exciting; thrilling and naturally satisfying when we feel it. Yet often it can be uncertain and illusive.

"Meaning" and that special sense of purpose in Life can also bring it, yet at the same time it can seem unrelated, connecting elements of the past, present and future to what in our minds choose to imagine or remember or even desire. And it holds in its hands the very gift of stability and comfort when at the end of the day our minds curl-up with the knowledge of who we really are in this life. When that curiosity has been satisfied, it adds to our sense of security. That is critical to our positive sense of Self, as it helps to validate our very existence. Only in knowing who we really are then and the deeper meaning of our Life can we find the comfort and peace we so desperately need. Over time, Carol came to recognize it, and so many of her questions were answered. Her Life was finally understood as she turned the pages of her own biography. It took great courage and perseverance. But she was up to the challenge. For Carol then, that look into the past was essential. It was vital she search for the understanding of all she was feeling as she peeled-back the experiences of her life over those years. There were times of happiness and fulfillment; moments of joy and even achievement. But what she had searched for in the end was an understanding of why she felt the way she did, and how those early years and experiences had impacted her sense of who she was. Her very identity and need for Jesus.

Everyone knows there are stories within a story, most often left untold. And so it is with the unusual and inspiring accounts you have read about through these chapters. They show both pain and suffering; deception and despair, and triumph over adversity. Hope's Journey was not written or set-out to be the end of Carol's odyssey - but rather the beginning of a new and inspired pilgrimage. When I first began to describe the life and times of this remarkable woman and through the very process of inquiry and letting the truth reveal what it inevitably will, I came to see new things in the struggle she'd faced over those extraordinary years. I would, with her help turn-over each and every event as the story began to take shape. And through those glimpses into the past, I became aware of more than the sum total of the parts of each experience. Sometimes there were new shapes to situations, and our talks helped re-discover feelings long forgotten; moments that had slipped beyond reach - until this writing.

"Often I was driven," she said, looking across the table in the warmth of the kitchen. I noticed her arm almost wrapping itself around the cup she still held, as if watching-over the thoughts that threatened to break-out if she were not careful. I couldn't help feeling the emotions that pushed themselves to the surface, and I wondered what particular event might have triggered the impulse after all we had discussed.

"Driven?"

"That's right. I felt driven. Pushed in a way I guess." She was silent for a few moments, giving me a curious glance before turning her head. Standing slowly, and struggling with some thought caught on a memory, she moved a few steps to the counter and lifted the pot of coffee. She filled the mugs and slid the jug of cream toward me. I thanked her and reached for the sugar off to the side. Her mood seemed to have changed and she was clearly entertaining a path we hadn't yet been down. But now was as good a time as any. .

Isn't it true? As individuals we find ourselves living in a world of uncertainty, struggling to feel safe and secure while trapped by the fear of being judged if we dare to be honest in revealing our feelings and the details of our lives. We mentally list our most important needs and set-out on the long journey of exploration, searching until we come to know ourselves for the very first time. Of course that is only the beginning. Yet only then do we better understand the reality of what had been facing us all along, and we see it perhaps a little clearer. Finally the pieces come together to give us a better picture of not only who we are, but WHY we are that way. Within this knowledge there is a certain freedom and some sense of relief when the awareness and familiarity make themselves known.

And although it is never quite enough to take away or hide the pain suffered through the difficult times, it can allow a momentary sigh of relief from the confusion that may have haunted us in our pilgrimage. That in itself can be very rewarding, giving us the confidence to look further and deeper into the past; to recognize who we are in the present, giving us the ability and the awareness to take responsibility for what and who we can become.

We often look to our past and say we are the way we are because 'this happened' or I made that decision because there seemed no other way. But we need to take responsibility at least to some degree for the decisions and choices we made that shaped our life and influenced our future. One day - even today will become our past; a past we can say inevitably directed the path we chose to follow. We just have to be aware of it. Many of us I'm sure ask why we don't use them; those convenient opportunities each and every day to help shape a future that is sure to come. But typically we can always find reasons for why we chose another way.

Reflecting on it, it's easy to say or think one is powerless to do anything about what has inadvertently come into our lives; the things and experiences that formed our characters and made us who we are. But the truth is, we always have power at some level, whether we recognize it or not. It's there. No matter how much or how little we have, we need to make the choice to exercise it. Even a little power, when used properly gains momentum and strength, like a snowball rolling down a hill. A ball once the size of a fist becomes a significant influence when given the chance. Used with wisdom, such a liberty is a positive authority that can be used to change our circumstances. The choice is ours.

The fact was, Carol came into this world on a cold Ontario morning under already stressful circumstances that would not only follow her, but would define who she was over the years. And her sister, a dozen years her senior, probably wasn't at all impressed with the new addition to the family. Understandably she would see it as more responsibility for her if mom was unavailable; either at work or simply busy with some chore on the farm. But that's just how kids think. It's a case of not only basic survival but also a competition for attention and resources which, when a sibling appears, has to be shared. Sure, we can always say it's just a part of grow-ing-up. But I used the word 'survival'; a word that is often charged with tension and curiosity for the reader as they look for an understanding to the difficulties facing a growing child. In fact, that search and even the interest and fascination helps move the critical events of the story into a place that demands more of our attention.

Within the depths of our curiosity along with well-intend-ed compassion we look for understanding of the pressures that influenced and pushed Carol into a place where any of us could be a victim. But lurking beneath the surface is a truth no-one can deny or even run from if we are to be honest with ourselves. We read and look into the life of another almost in an act of voyeurism with a focused intrusiveness that allows us to compare our own experiences with those of another. We tend to live-out our own lives like spectators in a gallery, wondering and living through the experiences of others without ourselves getting hurt. We observe behaviors and the fallout from the conflicts we are privy to. And we desperately need to know the outcomes as if viewing gladiators in the arena of life. The reality was, for Carol there was a particular need, given all she'd faced as her life unfolded. And that need itself was reduced to and described by a single word again: survival. And survival at all costs.

As much as I possibly can, I want to avoid going into Maslow's hierarchy of needs in any detail, and in fact it is out of the realm of this volume. But to borrow from his famous pyramid might just shed more light on the circumstances surrounding Hope's Journey. A child's first needs are physiological with its obvious meaning. But following that is the issue of safety - and later the need for love. To be loved of course is essential to our sense of well-being, as is our desire to belong and feel accepted. But the reality is, so many of us are missing more than one of these critical conditions from the very beginning. And that is essentially a situation that influenced Carol from a very early time in her life. But as with most who are missing any of these needs, she wouldn't in any way have been able to identify it alone. But she would feel it. And the loss would be carried by her through the years as she searched for satisfaction and the filling of each and every condition.

From the start, after the first time Carl made his move into her innocence at the tender age of thirteen, she knew what had happened even emotionally. She knew all too well how the dynamics were changing within the family as time went by because of the affair - which she certainly didn't engineer. She was just a child. She was not responsible for all that unfolded over that period of time - for the hurt it might cause to those around her. But the reality was, she had in fact been raped by the boyfriend of her sister, where not only her youth and childhood were compromised, but so potentially were the relationships within the family. In the silence of her deepest thoughts it was strangely cruel and frightening. Nothing would ever be the same again. And even at that young age she was conscious of what had been let-loose amongst them, and she would be torn apart with the intense guilt of it.

She found herself on a slippery slope, emotionally, grasping at anything that might give comfort and hope - or even safety from all she carried in her heart. Slowly she would start to see in greater detail the impact it could have if the family ever became aware of what had happened that night as the house slept. And it wouldn't allow her a moment's peace. Carol adored her sister; respected her and looked-up to her. She was an amazing woman, and her presence in Carol's life was critical for that sense of belonging. She needed her desperately as a young woman growing-up. But with all that had happened, she feared she could so easily lose her; lose her respect, and even her love; that much-needed love and the comfort it gave. It was a devastating time for her, and she lived with the guilt alone, not being able to share it out of fear. She was consequently forced into a place that knows its own loneliness and that could not be shared lest the truth leak-out. For all intents and purposes, it was to be a life-sentence into a silence that imprisoned her heart, mind and soul. Approaching her sister was out of the question. There was so much to lose, and not just for her, but for others dear to her, and she decided long ago to hold onto the secret. But it would take a dreadful toll over the years and influence how she would respond and interact with the world around her.

From an early beginning, even with a strong family support system in place, the metamorphosis a young girl struggles with through adolescence and into adulthood can still be a mind-boggling journey. The physical, psychological and emotional changes she has to deal with can be overwhelming. But for Carol, such support and encouragement wasn't even in the picture. That essential safety net we all need to move forward with confidence wasn't there. In effect, she was alone with the experience, with no-where to turn for help or advice. It must have been a very frightening time. And given her age where she was trying to make her way into the world of the adult, the sign-posts were missing; as visibly unavailable as was the love she had craved from a very early time. Now more than ever she needed to know herself - her identity as she grew into a young woman. But making that move successfully without an adult she could feel close to would be questionable at best. That special personal need goes far beyond the theoretical. And so, missing that essential connection would leave her no choice but to turn to others - even her peers for the validation she so desperately needed both through and after adolescence. In Carol's case, she had become unusually close to the man who had seduced and sexually assaulted her, creating a particular psychological dependency, and for all intents and purposes, he would become the one she would have to trust, and his values would over time naturally color her own to some extent.

Regardless, it was not enough to take away the guilt she was feeling as she allowed herself to become close to the man who would become her brother-in-law. Truth was, she was still a kid. And missing the foundation she needed to give her the vision and the strength - or find the wisdom to see her way out. As she matured, the guilt and shame went with her, weaving itself into every corner of her existence.

In her twenties she sought help from more than one therapist, but in the end, she was left with only the rudiments of an understanding of why she struggled with certain aspects of her life - especially relationships. She had lost the ability to trust - and to truly feel worthy of love; true love that would endure through any challenge. And there was always the liability of the awful experience with that man, for it colored every part of who she was as a human being - from her personal life, relationships and even her work. It clawed at her; reached for her through the moments and hung-up in her thoughts like a menacing burr. And she would feel the grip; re-live the moments that had caused her such grief and hurt. She would be driven by the transgression of that event for the rest of her life.

To maintain a status quo; an acceptable level of comfort within the family, she had been advised to hold back from confiding in her sister. And thinking it through, it made perfect sense to her at the time. There was the potential of too much hurt; broken relationships and a divided family. It was really impossible to even guess at what might have happened to them all should she have divulged the story to her sister. She loved her too much and couldn't begin to entertain the possibility of seeing her hurt. It was like a tragic play, and Carol was the main character. The happiness of so many depended it seemed on her maintaining her silence, even as an innocent child, and that heavy responsibility would be overwhelming at times, taking a dreadful toll. But she would hold to her decision and continue to suffer the guilt that plagued her every day with thoughts of the part she had played in an unintended deception. Speaking-out was simply too highly charged and dangerous. And she wanted more than her life to keep everyone safe and connected.

And so it was. While feeling she had little choice but to remain voiceless and endure the thought of all that had transpired, she lived with it daily, working around the feelings, doubts and even the confusion of how her life had been changed from that brief encounter. Now she was caught in a web. Trying to make amends or even fully understand the position she was in seemed impossible.

The very idea of guilt suggests a particular awareness to the fact that an individual could well have caused unimaginable distress to another. Shame by comparison describes or reflects a set of feelings about ourselves. And in many ways this is the greatest challenge to the sufferer for there is no escape. No matter how often the individual offers an apology, even mentally for whatever offence they see as having caused, they are still left with thoughts about themselves where they imagine they are quite dishonorable or even 'bad'. It is an almost impossible position to overcome and can and does consume much of the joy they may experience on Life's journey until it's put to rest. And she would struggle and try to escape it through a life designed to forget or even bury the past. Shame is perhaps the most difficult to deal with long term. It drains the very soul of its inherent goodness and strength. There remains little sense of safety or even belonging when the mind takes-on the task of judge and jury. And with this, only God can give comfort. The sense of independence though, or lack-of can lead to a feeling of disconnect in those special close relationships. And self-esteem, freedom and trusted affection may also be rinsed into nothingness from the despair that's experienced.

The fact is, making sound healthy decisions in life depends a great deal on one having a strong sense of self-worth and an obvious self-esteem. This was missing for Carol. The lower the esteem or self-acceptance, the greater the chances of making decisions that are not in one's best interest. Esteem implies the real authentic liking of oneself which gives a certain strength and confidence to the individual. When feelings suggest less than this, it can lead to a sense that sex is all a woman may have to offer at that point in her life, often given reluctantly to some who really don't understand them or their predicament. It is just the cost of "love" - a "pay-at-the-door" kind of love that has its own place. And anyway, 'explanations' would be avoided. Even hidden in the privacy and pain of the heart.

For others, 'intimate' affairs that are both physical as well as emotional can appear to help to an extent in raising self-esteem and self-acceptance at least on a temporary basis. An individual may become aware of a need they see and experience in others, perhaps a need they recognize in themselves, and confidence in one's sexual power carries with it its own strength and particular fulfillment. Still, with feelings of reproach focusing inward, it more often leaves one struggling in a very personal way to survive and fit into the world around them. To achieve this, some may react to stresses in ways that would or could induce feelings of greater value. Such a victim - because that's what they are - may be driven to acts of self-sacrifice - giving too much of themselves to those around them to make-up for any wrong they perceive they have brought about. Some might withdraw into themselves to escape dealing with the hurt they continue to feel, while others may look for power or authority in any capacity, making great effort to achieve a level of perfection in areas of their lives. Sadly, most often it becomes metaphorically a bridge too far, for it can never really be achieved. In the end, it all simply helps to describe and explain the depth of the anguish and suffering a person can find themselves coping with. One has to survive. And that's what it's all about. In a world so full of judgement and bitterness, it can be a terribly painful and lonely journey without the support of those people critical to your happiness and peace. And seeing someone, someone whose innocence was taken from them while so very young is difficult indeed.

A young girl, brought-up on an Ontario farm found herself at an early stage in her life feeling desperately unloved. Emotionally abandoned in some way. And as the needs grew while she worked to make the best of her circumstance, she was victimized by someone much older and wiser who had his own desires and issues to deal with. But the events that unfolded caused a young girl to make choices that would help her survive, no matter how good or bad they were. Some were good choices - but others would throw her into conflict as time went by. Regardless, all that came about from that experience and the monumental health crises she later faced sewed yet another unexpected panel onto the tapestry of her life - one that she would somehow learn to accommodate. We see once again there truly are so many stories within a story. Deeply personal and sometimes tragic. And, appropriately thinking back to that reference of "The naked City" - this has been one of them.

Whatever may have happened over those years to this child who would become a woman in search of herself, brought her to a point which would eventually lead her to God. From that place, so many answers would fall into line the closer she came. And she would come to know a new reality and a different understanding of not only who she was, but why her journey had taken her so far into the wilderness. Through a stream of dramatic circumstances, and in a sense of great desperation, she would call on Him. From that moment on, and because of her faith, it was just a matter of Time.

Through those early years, Carol didn't have access to a really caring parent who was truly 'available' for her psychologically and emotionally. And realistically there were many reasons for this as research and patience shed more light onto so many family events and situations. Over time, and after her own experiences with the challenges of Life, she came to understand that her mother who she loved dearly was perhaps in her own way doing the best she could under very trying circumstances. She too, along with her husband would toil to make ends meet. She worked hard to maintain the home, also finding a job away from the farm, and the days would have been long and tiresome. She too would have at times felt the exhaustion from her labor, and the stress of demands once home with a growing family.

While often not recognizing the efforts and contribution of her sons and daughters; while not seemingly even showing the love she must have held for each of them, she no doubt expressed it in her own way through her giving and doing; through work and the determination to do the best she could. There is little doubt her own needs were not being met either. But perhaps it better describes a woman; a mother who in her own way was struggling to survive herself against the odds. She was dealing daily with family needs a young child couldn't even begin to imagine, for obvious reasons. But that reality didn't change the fact a young girl was looking for the affection she needed to keep her on track and grounded. She was missing that critical connection with a parent. She needed desperately to feel the love of a mom and a dad; to be validated and understood. She needed to know just how important she was to the family.

Dad too had much to contend with on the family farm. It also was a time when, as described earlier, family farms of the kind we imagine seeing in movies, or reading about in stories were fading out of existence as the production of food became heavily industrialized across North America. Money had to be found. And that meant, at that time having to leave the farming lifestyle he had known and find work elsewhere in construction. It meant, unfortunately leaving home sometimes for weeks at a time.

A separation of that sort can heavily impact a family as they struggle with life; with school and simply growing-up. It brings with it, its own stresses and challenges; differences and frustrations. It steals the intimacy essential to the very heart of a family, often resulting in rifts and disagreements amongst the adults, and confusion for kids trying to find their place in the sun. They may feel their existence is not even really valued; that they have little worth around the home, or anywhere-else for that matter and it leaves them with a feeling of inadequacy and low self-worth. It leaves them also with very little sense of identity which in itself can be devastating.

So, now we know the full story of Carol's coming to know God, and how it has changed every aspect of her life since that cold February night in 1999. And it continues to do so today. Looking back, it's exciting and deeply encouraging to see so many of the things God has changed in her life; things perhaps she wouldn't have dreamed possible a few years before. In telling her story, as painful as it often was, she reflected on every facet of her growing years and even beyond; the memory of leaving home for the first time and more. In her search for answers she had scoured her thoughts and no-doubt those of others as she tried to understand the feelings she had struggled with for so long. And at last she did. But it had been a long and at times a dangerous and difficult journey. Still, the rewards continued to make themselves known in ways that left her at times speechless and in awe.

Through many trials Carol had found her way to God.

And after a few years with these changes so well established in her new life, she found herself one day talking about Christ and The Bible; about scripture and the promise of Eternal life when her mother and sister were down for a visit. Again His timing was perfect. And what unfolded was a gift of love she might have at one time hardly thought possible. But she had hope. And she had faith. After spending time in conversation with both about how coming to know Him had changed her life, her sister - then her mother both began to see the truth. They saw the light. And one Thursday evening in May of 2016, Mom was baptized in the name of Jesus at Carol's church in a semi-private ceremony. What an incredible day of celebration for everyone. And weeks later, her sister also committed her life to Christ. She too was baptized on her next visit to the city. The blessings were pouring-out and the bells in Heaven surely rang as His name was praised in a chorus of hallelujahs.

But there are still things that need to be told; thoughts, emotions and experiences disclosed before we leave her story. There was in fact much more to come over a very short stretch of time, and its telling will astonish even the most committed and adventurous reader.

Chapter Twenty-Five

GOD'S GIFTS PUT MAN'S BEST DREAMS TO SHAME

(Elizabeth Barret Browning)

SINCE CAROL BEGAN ATTENDING CHURCH ALMOST 20 years ago she had hoped in time her husband too might take that same leap of faith. As it was, although he had in his own way supported her commitment, he was never able to express any real interest in searching for God. Perhaps he was suspicious as many are. Perhaps he even doubted the reality of His existence, although that seems unlikely. Then it could have been a fear of taking that step because of a misunderstanding in perception of the Christian walk. But over time, things took an unexpected turn as you will see.

Dave had in fact suffered from certain health issues all his life, but severe back problems as well as problems with his neck were coming to a head by the spring of 2017. It affected every area of his life, and working in an industry where physical strength was essential was becoming increasingly difficult. His job required not only heavy lifting, but also climbing ladders with equipment and heavy tools tied to his belt. But it had all taken its toll and now he was really suffering terribly with pain which was at times excruciating.

Something had to be done if he were to continue working as he had for all those years.

You'll remember from an earlier chapter, both Carol and Dave had been to the medical centre of Sanoviv in Mexico for treatments described in those pages. And given his deteriorating condition in the Spring of 2017, it had to be addressed again as quickly as possible. Once more they'd searched for help in Canada but couldn't find the treatment, support and direction they were comfortable with. As a result, they decided to make the trip once again to Mexico where the medical staff had proven themselves capable and at the cutting edge of technology and new techniques. After first consulting with specialists there, and being encouraged by what was suggested, they trusted Dave's difficulties could be successfully addressed with a program they had in mind over a two or three week stay. Dave was scheduled for an MRI shortly after arriving at the hospital. Unfortunately, due to his severe claustrophobia, the attempt failed as he was unable to be moved into the tube for the procedure.

The next day, after meeting with the doctor, another appointment was made, but this time Dave was completely put out for the procedure. The MRI images revealed four herniated discs in his back; something which was definitely not expected. However, it gave a much deeper insight into the reasons for his back pain. Through consultation with the physician, there was nothing further they felt they could do, BUT rather unexpectedly, the doctor added there may be one other option that has not been considered yet. They had been seeing great results with stem cell therapy and there was a doctor in Tijuana that has been performing this procedure for over 20 years with great success. Dave and Carol felt naturally very excited with the news, and from what they had read and studied, it sounded like an excellent idea, showing promise of healing his body and renewing his strength generally. It was a most appealing thought, and they both felt encouraged by the plan.

Stem cell therapy is the use of a particular class of cells that may help treat a disease or even repair some other condition in the body such as arthritis or neurodegeneration amongst others. In that sense they serve as a repair system and at least theoretically can divide without limit to replace or replenish other cells where necessary. When a stem cell divides, each daughter cell has the potential to either remain a stem cell, or become another type with a specialized function such as a heart or brain cell. For Dave, the stem cell treatment suggested was designed to help with the pain suffered in both his neck and lower back, with the added benefit of helping restore full function to the vertebrae there. But actually there was the possibility of more.

Stem cells were eventually harvested from his stomach area and processed in the lab in preparation for the procedure later. Once everything was ready, the stem cells were injected into his neck, lower back and sacroiliac joint where one of his most painful troubles had started. The treatment itself, which must be completed with extreme care, didn't take as long as expected, and after waiting a further twenty four hours they returned to Canada feeling very hopeful that Dave would finally be pain-free. Time would tell as it took a considerable period for the stem cells to rebuild the tissue.

Once home, and naturally relieved at being back, he still needed time to rest and fully recover from the experience at Sanoviv. But he was heartened by all that had unfolded over the three weeks at the centre and felt confident with the promise the therapy held. Unfortunately, on April 26 Dave began experiencing chills and it was thought that perhaps he was coming down with the flu. With the benefit of over-the-counter medication, and care from his wife he seemed able to control it to some degree, but only for short periods of time. The fever would settle, but through the night would begin again with a vengeance. On the third day, late at night it began again, and went out of control. With the fever raging, and fearful of what it could mean, Carol felt she had no choice but to call an ambulance which she did on the morning of April 28. Dave was in trouble. The chills were so extreme he was shaking uncontrollably and violently; his lips turning purple. The anxiety and apprehension that gripped them at that moment was overwhelming, realizing for the first time just how serious the situation might be. Within what seemed like minutes Dave was transported to the hospital with Carol in close pursuit. They could never have imagined the difficulties and the suffering they were about to face.

Upon arriving at the hospital they immediately administered morphine for the extreme pain. And after a thorough examination at the hospital emergency department he was admitted for further tests, while his wife stayed with him through every step. As the doctors tried to stem the fever and look for a cause, there were endless questions for both of them, including a need to know what they'd recently been through out of the country; the procedures and findings of the team at the Sanoviv Medical Centre in Mexico. Wisely, Carol, thinking ahead had taken with her all the records from the facility there, including reports and an MRI so they could see for themselves how they'd approached his condition, as well as the treatments and medications given. Now, testing was on-going and extremely stressful for Dave and for Carol. And soon they would be both physically and emotionally exhausted with all that was unfolding after their recent ordeal.

Being back in Canada they were naturally excited, feeling the worst was behind them. But it wasn't to be so. The doctors at the hospital struggled to make sense of the pain and fever he was grappling with, becoming highly focused on the problem for there were so many possibilities to be considered; so many red flags to investigate. It must have been immediately obvious to his medical team that finding answers to Dave's dilemma would not be easy by any means. They would be challenged to navigate their way through what was to come.

During the first few days they worked to get his fever under control with antibiotics as well as medications to help with the intense pain he was in. It was unbearable and brutal, often driving him to his limit. He was literally in agony and soon they began to fear the worst, suspecting his suffering was somehow connected to the therapy received south of the border. Every scenario was being considered by the team taking care of him. The reality was, being wracked with pain and fever; his body was in extreme distress from what appeared to be an unidentified infection. Even time itself was becoming a problem in terms of his treatment. By now, Dave was barely functioning as he also battled a severe reaction to the strong medication and whatever infection was taking over his system. In fact, his very life was being threatened, and although his caregivers were protective and careful with their explanations, they made every effort as well to avoid mentioning there was a chance he may not win this fight. Of course, without question, in the event of the inevitable, they would have come forward.

The morning after his arrival at the hospital the doctors said they needed to send Dave for an MRI immediately as they had no idea what they were dealing with. This would provide another piece to the puzzle that was critical in administering effective treatment. But there was a problem. From the experience in Mexico, Dave could not possibly handle the procedure without being put completely out. After advising the doctors of this unfortunate limitation, they said it could take weeks to schedule an anesthesiologist. But that was not an option as time was already critical for Dave. The only alternative was to medicate Dave with selected drugs that would place him in sucha state he would not be coherent enough to know what was happening. One of those drugs was Hydro-Morph, a drug that often came with severe side-affects for some. In that sense then there was a risk, but it was felt there was no other choice as it still wasn't known what trauma they were dealing with – nor how to treat it. The doctors were naturally concerned that if they did not get answers quickly, there could be tragic consequences.

They started Dave on the I.V. with the drugs and scheduled the MRI for the next day. Concerned, and with that procedure in mind, Carol called the church and asked for urgent prayer. Within a couple of hours a gentleman from the congregation called, saying God impressed upon him they should meditate on the scripture, 2 Timothy 1:7 (*For God has not given us the spirit of fear, but of power and of love and of a sound mind*). They prayed, meditated and committed the scripture to memory, repeating it throughout the MRI test and the following day as the entire church added their support. Carol had asked the technician if she could go into the room to be with her husband throughout the procedure but the response was an adamant "No, absolutely not, it is against hospital policy for anyone other than the patient to be in the room at that time. You can watch him from out here."

For the duration of the MRI, and outside the room, Carol prayed and Dave repeated the scripture as best he could considering his state of mind. It was the longest 45 minutes of their lives, but it was a success and they now had the images they needed to make a decision of how to proceed with his treatment.

The following morning the doctors met with Carol and Dave, confirming an infection in the spine, not unlike Osteomyelitis, which is a form of bone infection. And although they were not able to identify the actual bacteria at this stage, they were better equipped to deliver a more focused antibiotic knowing finally the nature of the infection and where it was located. It was in the lower spine; actually in the SI joint in the lumbar area, and was also abscessed; contributing to the pain he was dealing with. Finding this was a huge step in trying to deal with his condition. In fact, after the team's search and destroy mission to find and identify the source, it was at last determined it had been introduced into his system most likely through the stem cell injections in Mexico. Whether a problem with a sterile field, or simply a slip in protocol may never be known. But this realization played a critical part in his treatment from that point on.

The infection though was not showing up in the blood and with no other clues available, they were still uncertain which antibiotic to administer. One alternative was to draw fluid from what appeared to be an enclosed sack at the infection site. But this was not risk-free by any means. The needle penetrating the sack could spread the infection throughout his body, and without knowing fully what they were dealing with, Dave could die. Only if his condition worsened would they take that risk. Dave's inflammation markers were very high and well over the normal range with the infection being severe and needing to be contained if at all possible. The pain was so severe by this time he could barely stand the sheets on his body. The slightest movement or touch on his skin sent waves of pain through him.

Initially, following the MRI, Dave seemed to be doing better and appeared at times quite humorous as he was still so high on the drugs. At one point he thought he was the commander of a space ship (he enjoyed watching Star Trek so this was obviously imprinted on him). But this humor soon worked itself out and in fact turned dangerous within a couple of hours of being settled again in his room. He became extremely violent, striking out at the nurses when they tried to treat him and manage his condition. Then someone suggested he needed to be restrained as he was a risk to himself, the nursing staff and other patients in the room. Before that could happen though, Dave was also struggling to get out of bed, while only a few hours before he couldn't walk or hardly move due to the effects of the medication. In fact, he really needed to stay horizontal and as still as he possibly could.

Given what the medical team was planning, Carol needed to give consent to the restraints they were insisting on, and at first she resisted initially for she knew how Dave would respond to them (and to her for allowing it to happen). The staff though assured Carol they would restrain him with only what was necessary for the moment, but something had to be done NOW. Reluctantly she signed the paper for them to go-ahead, and through tears, watched them fetter her husband to a chair that was fitted with a tray to prevent him from getting up. Regardless, within the space of 15 minutes, he managed to wriggle his way out of it and was soon standing on the chair and preparing to jump. The nurses did what they could to calm him, however, but had no choice but to call security. Within minutes, three security guards were in the room trying to hold him down. Dave was unexpectedly strong through it all and was immediately moved to a private room with much resistance. The intent was to increase the level of restraint; to make it more secure for Dave, and thus safer. Surprisingly, his mobility and strength were too much for the security guards to manage and they simply left him in the private room, watching from the window until he calmed down. Dave was swinging from the bathroom door and jumping off the bedside table onto the bed. He was completely out of control. Security quickly needed to form a plan of how to further restrain him, while the nurses gathered whatever apparatus they could find to contain him. Carol looked on in horror, knowing this could not end well. At this time, the infection was secondary and all action was taken just to get him through the severe side-effects of the drug.

Finally, the security guards entered the room and managed to get Dave onto the bed and into a system that would limit his movement even more. While better than the chair method, it too failed. In addition, Dave had now pulled the IV from his arm with his teeth. He was having no part of this and continued to act out violently, kicking and punching the nurse and disturbing everyone around. Security was called again as the immediate staff were unable to control him. Carol herself was overwhelmed with what she was witnessing, seeing her otherwise calm and gentle husband acting-out with such violence. It was a nightmare she could not believe she was living. The look in her husband's eyes was more like that of a wild animal; a look she only witnessed one other time in her life when she herself was at the end of a fist from her abuser when in her teens. She knew he needed to be restrained, but couldn't believe the aggression she was seeing from such a gentle and loving man; a man she knew could never be violent, except perhaps when cornered due to his claustrophobia. Before her very eyes a real-life terrifying experience was unfolding, and she could not believe the horror of what she was seeing.

It was now necessary to take the most severe step in re-straining Dave. As the nurses explained what they were going to do, Carol broke-down and wept. She knew it was necessary but continually reassured the nurses, this was not her husband. He was not a violent man. He was gentle and loving and deeply compassionate. She had never seen this behavior toward another person, ever. Regardless, they proceeded to take Dave's hands, securing them together with a strap while attaching the same to another belt that was secured around his waist. Finally, taking both feet and fastening each leg to the sides of the bed, Dave lay there, living out his nightmare, one of which he had previously told his wife he could never bare; the thought of being physically and totally restrained. After an intense struggle he was finally fully secured and safely held down. A long night lay ahead until the drugs finally left Dave's system, but it would be a frightening ordeal for him. All he could do now was beg for help. And that he did. All night long he called for Carol. He called for his brothers, Rick and Danny, He called for Carol's brother, Andy. But none came.

Carol never left Dave that night. While she didn't spend those dark worrisome hours at his bedside as she had the previous three nights since being admitted, he was still never out of her sight. In fact, while only a few feet away, she felt God was holding her back from entering his room. She had prayed, and sensed strongly the presence of God and His restraint of her. But she was still confused and so terribly distraught. She could not understand why God would not want her there at her husband's side while he was experiencing the worst night of his life. It was the hardest thing she's ever had to bare, seeing her husband, helpless, crying for his wife to help, begging. But still Carol could not go. She felt herself guided to stay close, but out of sight.

By this time Carol was not only confused, but totally exhausted, spiritually drained and fearing what would happen in the morning when Dave was lucid and finding himself still restrained. Deep in thought and hurting inside, she walked a short distance down the hall to call her Pastor and his wife. They were in Florida at the time, but by 1:00 in the morning she needed spiritual support, someone to talk to and pray with to get her through the long night. In the phone conversation that followed she was assured this was not a physical battle but rather a spiritual one. She believed with all her heart the need to maintain her distance from Dave for the moment, as God had impressed on her. Still she couldn't control her tears and wept openly while they prayed. When she did hang-up, she was left with the most encouraging words of strength and hope, putting all her trust in God.

When Carol returned to her chair that was positioned just outside Dave's room, she could see him clearly, but thankfully he was unable to see her. Through the night, she prayed, wept and trusted God. That's all she could do really. There was no one else she could lean on at this time. This was now in God's hands though she felt such apprehension through the night of what she would face in the morning when finally going into his room. The minutes ticked by, the hands on the clock seemed to stop. Already exhausted after three very long days at his side, Carol struggled. The nurses repeatedly suggested she go to the visitors room down the hall, take time out and just lay down on the couch. If she fell asleep they promised to wake her if necessary, but she refused to leave, desperately repeating how gentle and loving Dave was. This was not her husband. The nurses reassured her that they understood and knew it was the drugs that had created the unusual and unexpected behaviour.

By 6:00 a.m. Dave had become completely still, and all that was heard from the room was the sound of the attachment on the restraint as he continued to spin it with his fingers. There was uncertainty as to whether he was thinking he could free himself, or because that's all his hands could do as they were tied to the belt around his waist. And even that was secured to the bed. For another hour, Carol prayed. She prayed for the courage to go to her husband; for insight into what she would tell him of all that had happened the previous night to explain the restraints. She was uncertain what he would remember; what he would think of her while questioning the need for his being tied-down. Carol had faced a lot in her early years including abuse, fear and insecurity, but this situation took everything she had. Finally, she got up from her chair, walked into the room and sat beside her husband's bed. She can't remember exactly what she said, but recalls plainly what her husband's response was: "You can have everything. The farm. The horses. Everything!" Carol responded, "what are you saying?" Dave repeated, "You can have everything. I'll leave. How could you leave me last night and let them do this to me".

Through tears of distress she replied, "Honey, we had no choice, you were a danger to yourself and the nurses. Security had to be called three times during the night. We had to restrain you. You were going to hurt yourself. You had a severe reaction coming off the drugs and you were not yourself. Please believe me, I would not have let them do this to you if it was not necessary. I never left you all night." Dave responded, "I called for you all night and you never came. How could you leave me?" Carol reassured him, "I never left you, I was outside your room all night watching you. I would never leave you."

More calmly, Dave now shared with his wife "When you never came last night, I called on Jesus to come help me. And He did."

Weeping even more, she now fully understood why she was held back from entering the room through the long night. If she had, her husband never would have surrendered to Jesus. There comes a time when we need to step back and simply 'let God'. She stood up, bending over her husband, kissed him on the forehead and just hugged him. Relief flooded over her as she remembered the seventeen years of praying, waiting, surrendering and trusting. Now, at a time when she thought for sure, the circumstances would have driven Dave away from God ... God drew him near. Jesus was present in the room that night, embracing Dave, loving him, reassuring him and healing him, spiritually. He was there.

After Carol recovered and the tears subsided, she simply said, "I love you. Thank you Jesus." She held Dave close, knowing The Lord was with them. He was there all along. And she remembered His promise never to leave us or forsake us. Later, she reflected on the scripture in Romans 8:35-39, for through its comfort, she had come to know Dave was already safe in the hands of Jesus as He whispered, 'Come'.

Who shall separate us from the love of Christ? Shall trouble or hardship or persecution or famine or nakedness or danger or sword? As it is written: For your sake we face death all day long; we are considered as sheep to be slaughtered. No, in all these things we are more than conquerors through him who loved us. For I am convinced that neither death nor life, neither angels nor demons, neither the present nor the future, nor any powers, neither height nor depth, nor anything else in all creation, will be able to separate us from the love of God that is in Christ Jesus our Lord.

Carol spent the next three hours explaining all that happened throughout that night, helping Dave understand there was no need to divorce her. She WAS there, and with Jesus all through the night.

"I love you and will never leave you," she said to him again, "especially when you needed me most. But you needed to cry out to Jesus last night. And He came to you." Carol explained further how she felt held back from coming to him when he called, and now she understood why. And finally so did Dave.

In everyone's life, sometimes unknowingly there will be circumstances when Jesus will call; will make His presence known. Often we feel almost a desperation within ourselves to know our creator . . . our Saviour. The truth is, Jesus loves every one of us. He gave his life on the Cross of Calvary for every person who has, and ever will live. He will never force anyone, but will be there when circumstances call you to surrender. We were given a 'free-will' by a loving creator; a free-will to choose; to surrender to a loving God and invite

Him into our life and into our heart. And when we do, however small the step, He will move heaven and earth to bring about a change in your life. A change you will never regret. Remember. He loves you.

Spiritually, Dave was now secure in the presence of Jesus, and there was a relief beyond words; a comfort almost impossible to describe. And while still by his bedside, Carol softly sang Amazing Grace as a peaceful presence fell on the room. She knew, even through all the suffering there was a divine purpose to it all. Now Dave too was safe. And together they would be strong enough to face whatever may come, and with Jesus by their side. At last, and as husband and wife, they were finally sheltered and secure in His hands, safe in His unfailing love.

Chapter Twenty-Six

SURRENDERED TO JESUS

THE REALITY OF DAVE'S PHYSICAL CONDITION WAS still in front of them and they couldn't possibly know what challenges lay ahead. However, with Jesus, and their trust in Him they knew they could now endure it. While Carol continually assured the nurses there was no need to keep the restraints on, they refused to remove them. She even pleaded, insisting she would take full responsibility. She knew her husband was now settled and there was no longer any risk of injury. Unfortunately, her request was again turned down. All Carol could do now was to make Dave as comfortable as possible through the ordeal. Finally, after the doctor had seen Dave and assessed the situation, they agreed to remove the restraints. The pain though had now returned and seemingly worse than before. The strain from the events of that evening had undoubtedly caused some issues. It was later confirmed during physiotherapy that Dave had torn ligaments in both his shoulders as a result of the struggle. Unfortunately, the new MRI did not provide any further help, other than to confirm the infection was localized entirely to the site of the injection given in Mexico. While the infection was sizable, it had not spread to the rest of his spine or into the blood stream, but they could still not identify the bacteria. As a result, they were waiting to see if the inflammation markers were coming down with the broad spectrum antibiotics they were administering. Over the weeks it had become a daily regimen of blood work watching for any changes. Days passed, markers were still high. They were not getting any worse, but neither were they improving.

The days and nights were long, and he suffered terribly through each hour, struggling to stay on top and fighting to maintain his strength. Carol stayed by his side night after night, day after day, bringing foods she thought would help him maintain an upper hand and giving both physical and emotional support. She herself, under her own particular stress was labouring to stay afloat and be there for him. It was a terrifying time for them, and they were both grateful as members of her church; the Pastor and his wife, as well as others, came by to encourage and pray with them. That priceless unconditional support meant so much to them both. Without it, the suffering, stress and uncertainty would have made for a very lonely and frightening walk. Within days the medical team needed to repeat the MRI to see if there were any changes in the spine. Dave and Carol knew it was not an option to repeat the drugs described earlier. She would not see her husband put through that trauma again. Now, with Dave being surrendered to Jesus, their confidence needed to be with Him and totally trust (1 Peter 5:7). They believed Jesus would bring them through this, and Dave would exercise the faith he'd confessed just a few nights before. They prayed and the church prayed, singing hymns of faith while remembering the earlier scripture, *"For God has not given us the spirit of fear, but of power and of love and of a sound mind."* They were trusting Jesus completely. This test again was something Dave had to face, a terrible claustrophobic fear that had plagued him almost all his life. But this time he was not facing it alone.

A little before the scheduled time Dave was wheeled down the long corridors with Carol holding his hand and repeating the scripture. Upon reaching the MRI room, once again she asked, "Can I go in the room to be with my husband during the test?" Surprisingly, this time the technician said, "Yes, we can arrange that". God was already giving the reassurance of His presence and His ability to bring about the required outcome. Before entering the room Carol was given strict instructions of what to do and ensuring all metallic objects were removed. Now with much relief they both felt a greater assurance they could successfully get through this MRI.

Finally, Dave was carefully transferred to the MRI machine while his wife continued to reassure him, reminding him Jesus would bring him through this. Conscious of his apprehension, they repeated the scripture to each other with Dave knowing she would be praying the entire time. It gave him great comfort too, seeing her there, close by. Soon the doors were closed and the technician said they were ready to begin. For forty five minutes Carol prayed, while often moving to the other end of the machine to continually fan Dave so the heat would not overwhelm him.

With the MRI complete, the doors opened and Dave was slowly moved from the tube giving a sigh of relief. They knew this was yet another miracle. Jesus had brought Dave through an incredibly difficult experience that would otherwise have been impossible. The MRI in fact showed the infection was no larger, yet it had not shrunk either. Blood work was on-going in the hope it could by now be identified. But it wasn't the case. It was still an unknown. The doctors, looking for answers, continued to seek input from the Infectious Disease team to better understand what their options were. It was a very real possibility they'd have to resort to surgery if the inflammation markers did not come down over the next few days, and surgery was very high risk, and an option they were not willing to exercise unless absolutely necessary.

They waited, but Dave's pain did not subside and he was still unable to walk or even move himself in the bed. He was completely reliant on the hospital staff and a very kind friend, Randy, who came to the hospital daily to do whatever he could to make Dave more comfortable, move him and pray with him. The nights were long and equally so, the days as they waited and worried. They would read the Psalms, praying and singing and waiting on God. They knew He was in control and needed to have faith and trust. God's ways are always higher than our ways and beyond our understanding (Isaiah 55:8-9).

Finally, the markers began to come down, slowly at first and then quite significantly. They ruled out the need to have surgery as the broad spectrum antibiotics were finally hitting the infection. They did not know how long it would be or what Dave's capabilities would be after the infection was gone. It had been over two weeks and Dave was unable to walk, barely move and the pain was still intense. Carol continued to stay at the hospital, around the clock. She would sometimes retreat to the visitor room for a couple of hours at a time but always came back to the room checking on him and rubbing cream on his back which was helping with some of the pain. When she was unable to use the visitor's room, she would sleep in the chair at his side.

Dave, unable to sleep from the pain, found the days long and stressful. Little relief came, no matter what he was given. Although it may have seemed too early, after a couple weeks, they were already beginning to discuss his release from the hospital.

However, he would have to prove himself capable of a little more mobility before that was possible. With this thought in mind, there was greater focus on working towards rehabilitating him over the next while, making sure the antibiotics were doing their job, and that his pain was basically under control. Randy's help would be crucial in the planning because he had the strength to lift Dave, when necessary, and bare his full weight. And fortunately he continued to visit daily, getting him out of bed and basically dragging him in a bear-hug to the bathroom while walking back-wards. Slowly, and over a short period of time, Dave was able to bare some weight on his legs, but still screamed out in pain when it all became too much. Still, he was improving.

After three weeks in hospital he was released but with another 6 weeks of the antibiotics through an IV at home. Before releasing him, however, one more MRI was ordered to confirm reduction of the infection in his spine. This one though would be longer as they also wanted to have an image of the head to ensure there was no other damage in the brain or further up in the spine. In fact, it would take almost ninety minutes to complete. Again they knew Jesus brought him through the last MRI, but couldn't help feeling apprehensive as this one would be twice as long, and the challenge of him being on his back for that time created some serious anxiety. The church, once again prayed believing God would bring Dave through, reciting the scripture that brought them peace and knowledge, knowing Dave had nothing to fear. Jesus was in control.

Carol again was allowed to go into the room with her husband. But this time, the MRI had to be stopped twice to remove him as he was getting uncomfortable and hot. Once more, with a very trusting heart and the support of his wife, he made it through this very trying ordeal. By now they both realized the need to exercise faith, and believe He will 'be there' when needed most. Dave now was truly seeing the faithfulness of God, knowing and feeling his sweet presence and love. His once critical situation was at last improving, and the scale of the infection was shrinking. Also there was no evidence of any infection in his brain or anywhere else. What encouraging news for them after all they had gone through. The infection was completely localized in the site around his SI joints. Praise God. And Dave was released shortly after their findings. But he still had a long road ahead with daily nursing care and related needs to be taken care of. Carol however found herself filled with the most wonderful thought by this time. It was so nice to have him at HOME.

While it would be months before real significant progress was evident after the treatment, at the writing of this chapter,

Dave is still unable to work a year later. It's true they do not know when he'll return to work. But they do know the one who is in control. "*We know that in all things God works for the good of those who love him, who have been called according to his purpose*" (Romans 8:28).

It took over 10 weeks for the infection to be completely gone, but the healing was only just beginning, as was the spiritual journey that Dave and Carol were now on TOGETHER. It was in fact hard to believe he'd made it this far after the terrible ordeal he had been through; that they had been through as a couple. Now things were really beginning to look-up, at least a little. While still aware of the fact the condition wasn't necessarily out of the way, and could still be a threat, there was more hope than before. Of course there would be times of doubt and worry; even fear and frustration. But the brighter days were slowly increasing as one week moved into another.

As with all things in Life, there were other things going on alongside the difficulties they'd experienced. By his hospital bed those weeks ago, Dave would remember the prayers of his wife, and others from the congregation. He remembered the hope and encouragement it brought him. And he recalled fondly the prayers of Carol's pastor and wife as they stood by, supporting him and Carol time after time. He had come all too close to leaving this world, his body wracked with a terrifying and unknown infection. Now he was believing more and more in the reality of a divine intervention.

After so many years avoiding any real relationship with God, over the days he began to express his inner personal feelings for the first time, and soon there was a change even he himself had noticed. He recognized the difference God was making in his life, and would share it with Carol through the minutes and moments of a slow but definite recovery. Carol was already feeling the joy of his sharing feelings that perhaps would have been too personal only weeks before. What was unfolding was nothing short of a miracle. Then there was a devastating disaster that hit them, and so many others, as if a bomb had exploded amongst them. They were informed that the beloved wife of the pastor had fallen at her home from a heart attack and a stroke. The church; the congregation was in shock and disbelief. Word went out for prayer and support for the family as individuals struggled with what was unfolding amongst them.

Once in the hospital, with family around, the physicians worked feverishly to stabilize her condition. And the struggle went on for days, with a distraught and exhausted husband trying to maintain his composure through such a trying time. Then, one evening at a service in church, there was a phone call to the remarkable man filling-in for the pastor. The news brought a silence to the congregation as he quietly told those in the sanctuary the pastor's wife had passed away. They had lost the woman who had done so much for so many. She had devoted her life to God's work and to a new vision for the church. So many depended on her energy and devotion, and on her total committment to helping all those in her church family. The loss of this great lady was overwhelming. In fact it was hard to imagine how the church and its leadership could move forward after such a blow. It was devastating for all, leaving so many questions to be answered as they grappled with the loss and grief it left within the community. The effects of her death were crippling, leaving some feeling lost and anxious in their grief. But over the weeks they rallied together, helping each-other to rise above the horrendous loss. They gathered to help and support the pastor caught-up in his own personal grief, realizing this man had lost not only his dear wife and partner, but also his best friend and 'right hand' help for his ministry. It was a deeply significant blow and would take considerable time to come to terms with all that it meant. As the months passed, they would pull together to attempt to 'normalize' the church experience, and continue to work toward the goal of the pastor and his beloved wife; the moving forward toward a new vision of growth, as God had laid on their hearts.

Without doubt the impact of her passing on Dave too was understandably dramatic and overwhelming, as it was for Carol. They had become very close, and the sense of loss they felt was almost paralyzing at first. Still, the faith and prayers of the pastor and his wife as well as others brought Dave to realize he was finally on the mend. And there was the added comfort of knowing through those early prayer times by his bedside, a Bible Study had already been planned. Naturally though, this would now have to be put on hold for a while. In fact, moving ahead with the weight of it all on the mind was difficult and painful. But move ahead they did, and progress was being made weekly, emotionally, physically as well as spiritually.

Although only a handful of weeks had passed since his being home from the hospital, the first Sunday he was feeling strong enough to walk beyond the confines of his home, Dave made a decision to go to church with Carol. It would be difficult with the steps and getting into a comfortable seat as he was still using a walker. His back was still extremely sensitive and painful at times when he had to move a certain way. But he made it, and every Sunday morning after, as well as the evening services and the Tuesday bible study. It was wonderful to be there amongst his new church family. He clearly had made a personal decision to know and follow after God and had surrendered himself to Jesus. And there could be no better place to begin this new walk than in church and with his wife by his side. Within a very short time he was going up to every alter call and spending time there alongside his loving wife. It was beautiful to see this new commitment unfold, and the opening of another heart. At times in the past, Carol must have thought it may never happen; this miracle that brought him to know God and to openly exercise his faith. It was in fact a new beginning; a new beginning for both of them.

On a hot Sunday morning in mid September of 2017, Dave and Carol walked into church as usual. While otherwise an ordinary day, it turned out to anything but. After the morning service and alter-call, they returned to their seats close to the front of the church. Some came over to pray with Dave with the laying-on of hands, releasing any sense of resistance he may have had. But he was encouraged and felt the guidance and love offered on his behalf. The prayer time was intense and focused, and surely he felt God's calling through this particularly close experience. Before the end of the service, he received the infilling of the holy spirit, with the evidence of speaking in tongues. What an awesome moment for someone who had just committed his life to Christ. Throughout the church, praises could be heard in celebration of a day and a moment in Time that would never be forgotten. For both of them there was only joy, gratitude, and an awareness that both their lives would be changed forever. Carol's dream of almost twenty years had finally become a reality.

But there was another critical step to be taken in his early walk with God; one that was essential to the Christian faith. With this in mind, it wasn't long before he was asking to be baptized in Jesus name. One's baptism is the ultimate act of obedience, showing the convert's faith in a crucified, buried and risen Saviour. The act of Baptism also signifies the believer's death to sin and the burial of one's old life. It is in fact a statement of a new Life with Christ; a new beginning in the walk with Jesus. On a bright Sunday morning; the tenth of December 2017, and with friends and family gathered around, Dave was baptized. It was an incredible moment for all, and especially for Dave after waiting so long for this to happen. What an exciting and wonderful day it was; another day that will never be forgotten.

None of us can truly know where our journey will lead, nor make sense of the dreams that play themselves out in the mind. And Carol never could have imagined how something so traumatic could have ended with such sweet assurance of a future secured in His presence. But together they reflected on the events, knowing now the hand of God was surely with them. It was at a meeting with the doctor after Dave's release that a comment brought them to think again of the experience they had been through: "If the antibiotic we had given Dave had not worked, he may not have survived the infection." It was a thought that months earlier would have been devastating as Dave's spiritual condition was not secure. But that had all changed, for now he was at peace in the knowledge his eternity with The Lord was safe.

We never know when our days on this earth will run out, but as hard as the suffering may be in this life, there is an eternity waiting that we must make secure. The only way to do that is to surrender to Jesus Christ, the one who gave his life for our sins. Without that simple act of Faith we cannot have that comforting peace, or know what our future holds. Eternity really is forever. Our decision in this life secures where we will spend that eternity; with a loving Savior who gave His life for us, or in an eternity spent separate from God and His promise of everlasting Life.

Carol's story; her journey if you will, has shown that through abuse, addiction, trauma and regret; through mistakes and misfortune and her eventual triumph over tragedy, she was brought to seek His face as she knelt in desperation that night at a secluded retreat. She saw a life for what it was, and knew at once she needed Him. Only God could save her and her future; her very Life in fact. She had seen the light and called out to Him in that critical moment of need. And we have seen the result of her prayers then, and into the present. So often, when near, you will hear the words spoken softly, "Thankyou Jesus."

Each individual then must make a personal choice to accept His sacrifice, made in our place for the sins all have committed. And perhaps now is the time to consider that very thing; to surrender and accept His free gift. To do so, we must repent of our sins, be baptized in the name of Jesus Christ through full immersion, and receive the infilling of the Holy Spirit (Acts 2:37-39). This is what is considered the new-birth experience. We must be born of the water (baptism) and the spirit (Holy Spirit – John 3:1-21). We must be born again.

And so it was. As she looked back, and as the years unfolded for Carol since she'd played on the hill of her grandparent's farm as a little girl, she would at times think of her childhood in a small Ontario town a stone's throw from the border of Quebec. She would remember the streets and the events that led up to the present, finding it hard to believe where her journey had taken her. The memories would at times be painful and difficult to think back on. At times she would comment, "I hardly recognize the former me. God has completely transformed me and the image has changed."

The sexual exploitation by a much older man. The abuse by others she'd dated, hoping to connect in a very human and loving way. The trust she lost and the experiences with the questionable choices made through her genuine naivete. The tragedies sprinkled with little glimpses of hope. The struggles to create a more fulfilling, rewarding and complete life. Her moving to a town in southern Ontario where her new life would begin. The successes of her professional career and years in management as well as her studies to gain a degree in Business. And then the realization of all she and her husband had been through together, and all they had achieved. In truth it was, and is quite remarkable and heartwarming. And all a gift from God. Of that she was convinced. And so now is her husband.

As I write this final section of Hope's Journey, and think on where it has led me the author as well, I'm prompted to think of a piece in Jeremiah which in so many ways sums up the thoughts that surely have been on their mind too after the events covered in this final chapter. And I believe it answers the questions so many of us ask about God; about finding Him. And Jeremiah 29:12-3 makes it clear:

"Then you will call upon Me and come and pray to Me, and I will listen to you. You will seek Me and find Me when you search for me with all your heart."

Now having reached this point, it's still not the end of the story, but again a new beginning for them and for so many others, including this writer. In its writing I too have been on a journey that took me where I could never have imagined. In the three years since I followed that simple star on a home-made map and drove down the long winding lane to talk with Carol, so much has happened on a personal level. And there is an added reason why I chose to call a chapter, "God's plans put men's best dreams to shame."

Over those days, months and years I came to know Carol very well. And then Dave. In fact it was Carol who gave my wife and I our own Bible Study in our home some five years ago. And we remained close friends from that point on. We would visit each-other, and over that time she would spend the occasional evening with us, sitting around an old familiar kitchen table while we talked and shared stories about God, about Life and events of the day. And we would meet in church, finding ourselves one day sitting together close to the front. It was a blessing in which I found great comfort and peace, and a closeness that was uniquely special. As our relationship grew, so did the familiarity and nearness after all that had been shared.

We believed what was unfolding was God's plans for us all, both individually as well as in the wholeness we had become. Over many occasions Carol and I shared thoughts and feelings about Life itself; about ambitions, dreams and relationships, and personal thoughts on families, affection and fellowship. An inseparableness developed and a devotion that transcended simple friendship, leading us to feel more of a family than acquaintances. It was from that seed that over a period of time we talked about our relationship as being like that of a father and daughter. Carol, as you learned from her story had lost her father while still quite young, and it was a relationship she desperately missed. And all that it could have meant.

Our conversations eventually led to thoughts on making a dream come true after the personal feelings we'd shared. It was a desire held in both our hearts for a growing number of reasons. After much time had passed, and with the full recognition of each spouse, and Carol's mother, it was decided we would carry it further and even consider my adopting Carol as my daughter. I had come to love her dearly as my own, and so the application was made through the courts. Within the space of a little more than a year, the decree was finally granted. God's blessing was with us. We had at last become a family. And another gift was celebrated. And so this too is a part of her story; a part of Carol's life. And now a part of mine and so many others.

Such then are the details of her own remarkable journey, with all the hills and valleys it entails, and at least some of the lives it has touched. It is a story of challenges in a search for happiness and fulfillment, and ultimately the search for God Himself. She found Him. And He saved her. But without her turning and surrendering to Him in her time of need, it could have had a totally different ending.

For so many years now Carol has called on him and He has always been there. He will be there for you too. With only the faith of a Mustard seed He will make His presence known. This in the end is what Carol had wanted to say to you, the gentle searching reader - to know and understand, no matter where you are on your journey; no matter what the circumstances, afflictions or uncertainties - reach-out. Believe. Put your trust in Him.

Hope's Journey is not only a story, it is also a testimony to how circumstances, challenges and dreams can drive us in our search to find Jesus, our God and Saviour. Yet it speaks eloquently with its own seasoned voice to what is inherent in the human spirit, and addresses the need for God in our lives. It's a voice that gives us the courage to seek His face against the odds; to have Hope, and embrace the words spoken in Jeremiah 33:3 - *"Call to Me and I will answer you, and I will tell you great and mighty things you do not know."*

His name is **Jesus**.

Past, Present. Future

Alone but not forsaken . . . He awaits

Life without direction . . . Hope and Journey are hidden from view

Empty, Desperate, Unlovable

When will it end? What is the Purpose?

Hope, the journey begins. . . All things come into focus

The other side of the pain

Appreciate all things . . . It was all a part of the plan

Regrets of the past . . . Greater are the promises of the future

My Saviour, holding His nail pierced hand

Solitude

The miracle of Love – Reborn

Prayer and worship

Purpose and vision – there are no borders

Entering the gates – Jesus will meet me there

All tears wiped away

The bright and morning star – Jesus

Eternity.

My journey taught me to feel the warmth of the sun and understand the face from which is shines. To look upon a glorious sunrise with awe and see The Artist.

To watch and smell the aroma of an opening rose and find the gardener there who fashioned it. To witness a butterfly emerge, knowing it had to die before living and could not fly without the struggle. To see the birth of a child and know the miracle who gave it.

To kneel in reverence of God when understanding His promise given in the rainbow.

To reach for the nail scarred hands and experience the love

that allowed it. To experience true peace, knowing and being known of the One who purchased it for me.

To surrender my life to Jesus today and every day, knowing His love is immense, unfathomable and unending.

To read and experience His word, I came to believe in the Hope He gives so freely.

Finally, every promise is true. I know, I am experiencing them.

Carol, November 13, 2015

About the Author

As an educator and author, Bentley-Drury was ecstatic when asked to write a biography powerful enough to change the life of the reader. And that's what he believed it could do if circumstances led them into their own search for under-standing; into a search to know themselves more fully. It was with this thought in mind he passionately took-on the task of its writing, bringing about an unexpected change in his own life through the process.

His earlier work included a novel, *The Mystery of Sand Lake*, written for use in the classroom, plays and a short children's story for language and vocabulary development. Most of his writing, outside of education has been nonfiction, focusing on events in people's lives; adversity, achievement and the challenging walk that eventually carried them into the sun-kissed fields of their dreams; into success and satisfaction, and a life of peace and hope. With a deep personal and professional interest in mathematics and language, literature and analytical juris-prudence, Bentley-Drury is married and lives in South Western Ontario with his wife and a playful, mischievous yellow Lab, saddled with a huge sense of Self, and personality 'to go.'

71129970R00170